WHITE
LIGHT

The Complete Guide
to Spells and Rituals
for Psychic Protection

To Pat,
in Love & Light

Diana Ahlquist

WHITE
LIGHT

The Complete Guide to Spells and Rituals for Psychic Protection

Diane Ahlquist

CITADEL BOOKS
Kensington Publishing Corp.
www.kensingtonbooks.com

CITADEL PRESS BOOKS are published by

Kensington Publishing Corp.
850 Third Avenue
New York, NY 10022

All Kensington titles, imprints, and distributed lines are available at special quantity discounts for bulk purchases for sales promotions, premiums, fund-raising, educational, or institutional use. Special book excerpts or customized printings can also be created to fit specific needs. For details, write or phone the office of the Kensington special sales manager: Kensington Publishing Corp., 850 Third Avenue, New York, NY 10022, attn: Special Sales Department, phone 1-800-221-2647.

First printing: February 2002

10 9 8 7 6 5 4 3 2 1

Printed in the United States of America

Library of Congress Control Number: 2001098933

ISBN 0-8065-2298-4

I dedicate this book with much love to two
people who are dedicated to me. My mother,
who instilled in me that anything is possible
and for her constant love and encouragement
in all endeavors. And the love of my life, Adrian,
for trusting and believing in me above and
beyond the limits of love.

CONTENTS

PART IV. DIANE'S PERSONAL DEFENSE TECHNIQUES

PART V. DAILY DEFENSE SYSTEMS

PART VI. SECRET REALMS BEYOND THE PHYSICAL (CAUTIONS AND WARNINGS)

ACKNOWLEDGMENTS

I have been very blessed by God to have so many incredible people in my life who have encouraged and guided me.

This book came into being because of the efforts and faith of Claire Gerus. She not only gave me a chance in the literary world, but also gave me the name of the book, *White Light*. To her I express heartfelt love, thanks, and appreciation.

Hugs to Sandra Scanlin and Dennis Dalrymple for their valuable information, faith, and guidance.

My gratitude to Joe Lubow, without whose help and excitement this book would not have found itself in the right hands. May the most that you wish for, be the least that you receive.

A very special thanks to my agent, Noah Lukeman, for his efforts and negotiations.

With the "Passion and the Purity of Angels," I will always be grateful to Dave Stern. His patience, pep talks, and guidance were always available. He shines light into dark corners.

Warm thanks to my dear friend Sandra Gentile. Her dedication and advice on this project were invaluable. Hours of reading my manuscript and her comments took much burden off me and gave me confidence to continue.

My sister, Marie Frenden, who also was an encouragement and loving energy in the writing of this book. May her passion for the people of Tibet and her journey to spiritual fulfillment be blessed with divine light. *Namaste.*

Finally, with love and thanks to:

Richard Ember, my editor at Kensington, for his patience contributions and open-mindedness to this project.

David Stahl, for the many journeys we experienced in Mexico and his support and wealth of information that contributed to my successes. Thanks, Andy.

Roger Goff, for his expertise on metaphysics and Reiki. His contribution to this book echoes through numerous pages.

Kathy Greager, for her calm energy and devotion to the world of the paranormal. A true friend.

Thank you to my contributors:

Ray T. Jacobs, DVM, for his written contribution on magnetic therapy and energy drain in Chapter 3: "Careers That Are Prone to Psychic Attack." Thank you for your professionalism, care, and knowledge.

My best to Kenneth Clark of Clark's Candlery LTD in Scotland, for his personal method of creating a black candle in Chapter 19: "Black Candle Ritual to Dispel Negativity." Your personal touch made the difference.

Thank you to Joe Lastowski, Jr., for his artwork within these pages, which brought clarity to what I was trying to express.

Additional warm thanks to:

My nephews, Johnny and Daniel Frenden, for accepting that their aunt was "a little different" and always being supportive and proud.

Inger Svenson, for her support beyond friendship. You kept me going when I needed to hear reassuring words.

To my friend and colleague, Ernest Sekunna, for his numerous readings using oriental astrology, palmistry, and his natural psychic abilities. Everything you predicted for me has come into being, Ernest. God bless you.

Kimberly Perkins and Lea Semple, for providing Sarasota with a place to gain knowledge and insights, as well as unknowingly introducing me to a person that would change my life. In love and light I thank you.

Blessings and gratefulness to: Garland Landrith III, Ph.D.; Mike Seery; Robert Irwin; Lori Frenden; Barbara Jones; George Avena, Minoy Downes and Pat Samuels.

To those who have passed, especially my lovely grandmother and grandfather. I thank all that continue to guide me from spirit.

To all others who have shared their experiences generously in this book.

Introduction

Our planet is in a constant state of chaos. Most of us experience more upheaval than tranquillity. We suffer from stress and low energy levels, and our bodies not being nearly as obedient as we would like them to be. Many of us just become exhausted and feel totally drained of our vital life force, not being sure of the reason.

In these modern times the medical world may call it chronic fatigue syndrome; the holistic world may claim it's too much manufactured medicine; and our great-great-grandparents may say we're just spoiled, lazy, and not used to hard work! I feel that all these beliefs have their place, but so does the theory of *psychic attack*. Psychic attack is an energy drain from people, places, or things and in very rare cases even the nonliving. These attacks cannot only deplete us of energy, but cause illness and confusion in our lives.

Individuals who have ill thoughts or intentions against us, willingly or unwilling, can put us under assault by means of dominant thought-forms. The people I suggest are not all evil and sinister but, for the most part, are ordinary people like your neighbors, coworkers, or family members.

Psychic storming can also emanate from places. A place or location can retain the vibrations of a past resident or corrupt situation. Things or objects also have the ability to collect menacing vibrations of a previous owner or predicament that was of an adverse nature. Consequently, they may transmit offensive echoes to all those who come in contact with them.

Clearly, we cannot avoid coming into contact with people, places, and things since we cannot avoid life. Therefore, we need a daily system of protection, as well as special and more powerful forms of protection for those periods when we may be hit with more intensity or by total surprise.

As a third-generation psychic born into a spiritual and intuitive family, I have witnessed a great variety of phenomena. Unfortunately, although my family was excellent at doing "readings," making predictions, and solving problems for people in times of despair, they were lacking in the area of practicing the forms of psychic protection that had been passed on to them through the generations.

It was only later in my life that my grandmother shared with me techniques handed down to her. When I asked why it took her so long to share these techniques, she claimed she didn't think we needed them because she never needed to use them. With all respect, what she did not realize was that she did not need them because she was a tough and stubborn woman!

I am convinced it was her sheer stubbornness against negativity and ill wishers that kept her protected. At times she had a very rigid edge, to say the least. And heaven help the person who directed ill intentions at her!

When in her eighties doctors told her it will be unlikely that she would be walking much longer, she waved her hand as if dismissing them and said, "What do they know?" When she finally passed away at ninety-four years of age, she had been walking with the use of only a cane!

At age ninety-two, she had also predicted her own death. She explained to my sister, Marie, that she had decided she would live for about two more years and that would be enough! Well, sure enough Grandma M passed away two years later. *She* decided whether she would live, die, walk, or not walk. With a powerful will such as that, who needs psychic protection?

Although my grandmother had her own natural form of defense (stubbornness), the rest of us were unguarded. To put it kindly, we were of a gentler nature.

Like my grandmother, I, too, had developed protective techniques of my own, but strictly out of necessity. When I was approximately ten years old, I was terrified by apparitions that walked my mother's hundred-year-old house and I devised a way to do what would now be referred to as "ghost busting." I never discussed it with anyone. Everyone just thought our visitors went away. I will explain how I developed this procedure in detail, in Chapter 5: "Ghosts."

When I was a teenager, someone put a curse on my sister and our entire family. We didn't truly believe in curses and were not very superstitious until circumstances continually got our attention. I lifted that curse. Once again, it was out of necessity with desperately strong intention. I will explain this as well in Chapter 4: "Hexes, Spells, and Curses."

As I grew to adulthood and investigated psychic attack, I shared my methods of psychic protection with others. Given their successful feedback, the theory of coincidence or delusion became more impossible to believe.

As I further researched the subject, I found other forms of safekeeping that our ancients used, such as symbolism, herbs, Feng Shui, and a variety of rituals and ceremonies. These I also include in this book. I refer to them as "Traditional Forms of Protection" (See Part III).

Other books and publications on the same subject have been written and I feel they all have merit. I have seen some authors strike out at or try to discredit others for their writings on psychic protection. This I will not do. If I were to attempt to belittle or negate the philosophy of someone else in order to make myself appear worthy, would I not be initiating a psychic attack on them? How could I project something I am attempting to help you guard against?

That being said, I hope you find some value in this book. Hold on tight to what you feel connected to and let go of what does not sit right with you. For those of you who enjoy my book, blessings to you, for those of you who don't, blessings to you anyway!

An Unplanned Story About Grandma M

This section of the Introduction was not planned or outlined. However, it does address psychic defense—but not from the living. In fact, it comes from the very woman I just wrote about—my grandmother—and as I write, my force fields are in place!

This is my fifth attempt to try to finish the writing of this

Introduction. My book is nearly completed and I cannot seem to get through the section referring to Grandma M. Months ago, I described her as a "human rubber band," who would spring back at you if you attempted to pierce her protective energy field. I did it without maliciousness but as a way to describe her personality.

Seconds after I wrote those very words, I decided to take a break. I went outside to talk to my fiancé, Adrian. The sunny skies here in Florida suddenly darkened and it began to thunder.

No ill weather was predicted and it was not rainy season. I made a joke to Adrian that Grandma must not have liked what I had written about her. We laughed and thought nothing of it. Again, thunder from nowhere! Adrian is not at all superstitious and does not believe that every little noise or unusual happening has a higher meaning. However, we both felt very uncomfortable. "Maybe you should take the part about your grandmother out of the book," Adrian said seriously. "Maybe I should," I replied. I went back to the computer and deleted those sentences.

Immediately the sun came out and all was normal. I left the Introduction for a later date.

Two weeks passed and I started to continue to write this Introduction. This time I thought I would refer to my grandmother in a gentler manner. Yet I had to get the idea across to my readers that she was tough and it was this toughness that formed her armor of psychic protection.

I used different words such as "determined" and sometimes "obstinate," and wrote, "Having had a hard life and living in those times, it would be no wonder why she was not as loving as she could have been." As God is my witness, my computer froze up! This was not a normal occurrence and it rarely happened as my computer was in top running condition.

When I got the computer functioning, my entire Introduction was gone. I made the decision to skip the Introduction for the moment and just continue with the rest of the book.

A month later I tried again, as I wanted to get the Introduction behind me. Once more, I needed to address the influence my grandmother had in my life, as she is the one who taught me how to develop my intuitive abilities, yet I wanted to be honest about her strong will.

In the meantime I had discussed these strange occurrences with my mother. "Oh." My mother laughed. "Your grandmother doesn't give up even from the other side! You better say nice things about her. You know when she was growing up in the nineteen-twenties, she was a beautiful woman, a real 'flapper.' Maybe you could put that in the Introduction."

Of course, my first response was, "What does that have to do with psychic protection?" My readers want to learn how to use psychic self-defense to enhance their lives; they will not be interested in whether Grandma M was good looking!

"Okay," my mother responded. "But if you don't say something about her looks, you will not get your Introduction written. You know your grandmother was vain."

"Oh, mother," I replied. "Don't plant seeds in my head. I'm sure I am just being paranoid or something."

A few weeks before the deadline of the book, I attempted to finish this Introduction.

Everything was going well until I decided to mention my grandmother could have been a secret weapon for the military, as by merely standing in the battlefield her aura was so dominant the enemy would have turned around and run! Will I never learn?

While typing, I leaned back to cross my legs to get more comfortable, as I knew I was finally making progress. Suddenly my sturdy office chair keeled over. As the chair fell on top of me, it hit my left wrist, leaving it swollen. So I gave up once again.

This is now my last attempt at this Introduction. Although a few days ago I suffered no serious injury, as I type here today, an elastic bandage supports my left hand.

Nevertheless, I believe I have made it through. Admitting defeat and never thinking I would have to protect myself from my own grandmother, I came up with a resolution. I protected myself with the largest "white light" I could envision. And by the way . . . My grandmother was a beautiful woman!

There. I just finished my Introduction!

Auras: The Basis of All Protection

White light is a protective light of life energy that you can utilize through thought and visualization. By applying white light techniques, you can break the bonds of the earthly laws of space and time. White light protection is the force field that negates psychic assaults and destructive vibrations that may attempt to penetrate your aura. In fact, it is a component of the aura. Of all the forms of protection that can be utilized for psychic preservation and maintaining a healthy psyche, the aura is the basic tool. It will keep you balanced and safe. With practice, you can control, change, open, or close it within seconds.

For years, people have used their auras to surround themselves with an armor of fortification against psychic warfare. It is this nonphysical shield that kept my grandmother safeguarded and strong. She may not have known the word for this protective shield, but this is what I later recognized it to be.

To develop a strong and healthy aura, you must understand what the aura actually is and how to read your own aura, as well as the auras of others.

The word "aura" comes from the Greek language and means "breath" or "air." It is an invisible emanation, an energy field that arises from and surrounds every person and living thing. We all have auras. If we do not have an aura, we are no longer alive.

Throughout history, artists depicted people such as Jesus Christ; Buddha; Mary, the mother of Christ; and other spiritual beings with crowns of light around their heads or entire bodies.

Your aura comes from within. To develop a strong aura, you must have balance in what I refer to as the "Auric Trinity": strength of body, mind, and soul. With this balance, no one would need any other type of psychic protection. It would be so powerful, nothing could penetrate, pierce, or permeate it. However, to have such balance of the "Auric Trinity," one would have to be nearly perfect, which few of us are.

It is difficult to have all three of these aspects aligned at the same time. We may have control over our physical self but need to follow a more spiritual path. We may be proud of the spiritual path we are walking, but need to work out our physical. We may achieve the physical and spiritual aspect, but need to use our minds more. It reminds me of juggling. We can toss two balls around in the air but when we try to incorporate a third, it becomes more challenging. Although auras are our best weapons against psychic attack, few have achieved an energy field that can not be penetrated. This is why in addition to our natural aura, we must use other means of psychic protection.

To understand the power of auras, I will show you how you can learn to see the auras of other people. By learning to do this, you will be able to see someone's feelings, intentions, or state of health before they even speak. If everyone on the planet could "see" these forces, we would never lie or be dishonest. All would know the truth through their auric sight. The aura does not have the ability to lie and we cannot disguise it and make it appear as something it is not.

Through this source we can detect the spiritual evolution of an individual. A glowing, clear emanation will indicate someone who is spiritually secure and compassionate. In the case of a darkened or gray aura, the person may be sickly and have many inner challenges to overcome.

To see an aura, one does not have to be psychic or have knowledge of some type of ancient wizardry. Children under the age of five see auras by nature, as their minds have not been restrained by external influences.

I admit, some special people do have a natural ability to see this unique indicator of moods and vitality much more extensively than others do. A gifted few can behold this forcefulness without any practice or guidance. This was the case with Edgar Cayce.

Edgar Cayce, America's best-documented psychic, known as

the "Sleeping Prophet" because most of his "readings" were performed in a sleep state, was always aware of people's auras.

Cayce wrote, "Ever since I can remember, I have seen colors in connection with people. It was a long time before I realized that other people did not see these colors; it was a long time before I heard the word aura, and learned to apply it to this phenomenon which to me was commonplace.

"I do not ever think of people except in connection with their auras; I see them change in my friends and loved ones, as time goes by—sickness, defection, love, fulfillment—these are all reflected in the aura, and for me the aura is the weathervane of the soul. It shows which way the winds of destiny are blowing."

Like learning a musical instrument or developing an art, with practice we can all develop the abilities to see auras on some level. Perhaps we will not all acquire the expertise of Edgar Cayce, but we can at least get the general concept of what we are observing.

To prove this point, I took a small group of ten adults ranging in ages from 21 to over 80, some of them skeptics and some openminded. None of them claimed they could see auras and none was aware of what the different colors associated with the aura meant.

Fifty percent did not believe that an energy field around the body even existed! And quite frankly, I had to plead with the skeptic group to be a part of this experiment.

I placed two people in front of them who were complete strangers to the group. Both were female, had the same color eyes, and were approximately the same age, height, and weight. They both wore the same T-shirts and blue jeans. I asked both to wear the same hats as to hide hair color and style and requested they wear no jewelry. There was no communication or eye contact with anyone in the group before this experiment.

Someone walking into the room would have guessed they were twins. One had health issues, financial difficulties, and romantic problems. The other was spiritually evolved, loved life, and had an outstanding lifestyle.

Before we began, I asked the women not to smile and to go as far as covering their mouths with their hands so as to not reveal the shape of their mouths. They both looked straight ahead at a picture on the wall.

Using the method to see auras, which I will describe a bit further on in this section, the entire group came up with virtually the same results. They saw the same colors and wrote down what they had seen.

Two of the skeptics and two believers insisted they could not see a thing. I told them to make it up, just naming any color on the list. The individuals who supposedly had to "make it up" chose exactly the same colors as the others. I believe subconsciously they did see colors but wanted to make a point or did not want to be incorrect.

When all was completed and the results were presented, the skeptics became much more open to the idea of auric sight. Having participated firsthand, they could not ignore the fact that the overall consensus of the group was the same. The color of the auric field around the woman with the more tranquil life had specific positive colors, as opposed to the other woman with trials and tribulations, who showed colors of negativity and need.

Scientific evidence of auras was provided in 1939, when a Russian scientist named Semyon Kirlian discovered that if an object on a photographic plate is subjected to a high-voltage electrical field, an image of the object's aura is created on the plate. This photographic process, known as Kirlian photography, is able to show the energy patterns in the aura. When a disturbance in the energy pattern is seen, it can indicate a disturbance in the organic structure of the photographic subject.

A whitish tone is usually the closest energy field to the body. Following the white we will tend to see the different hues. Your auric colors change with your moods and your health. If you were to have your aura photographed before and after a well-deserved vacation from your workplace or obligations, you would see the uplifting change in colors, providing your vacation was relaxing and not more stressful than your work. After the holiday your auric colors would most likely show healing and be clearer.

Tranquillity will show itself with a glistening and large energy track. Ill health or depression leaves us with an energy field that is pale and narrow.

The auric colors that we see give us a vast amount of information about the bodies, minds, and spirits of others and ourselves.

For centuries we have associated colors with our frame of mind.

"I can see you've been blue lately." "She was green with envy." "I was so angry I saw red!" You probably already know, feel, and see more than you realize about color and the aura.

Developing the ability to read another person's aura is in itself a form of protection, as you will then be able to know what the disposition of any given individual may be. If I walk into a room and see a group of people with weak or dark auras, I usually plan a way of leaving as soon as possible. I remove myself before anyone even notices that I was there. It is almost like a secret radar system that gives you forewarning of danger and future jeopardy. This is why it is so important to take the time and effort to begin to read auras.

How to See Another Person's Aura

Find a friend or loved one who is open-minded and willing to be serious about this experiment. Choose a time of day and a place where you have privacy and no spectators.

1. Have the person stand or sit in a chair in front of a white background such as a sheet or wall. Stare at the middle of your subject's forehead—the third eye. (In ancient times, people in countries such as India and elsewhere put a mark on their forehead—distinguishing the third eye—as a type of an invitation to look into their aura and "see.")

2. After focusing at that spot on your partner's head for approximately thirty seconds, examine the area with your peripheral vision. Remember to keep your focus on the spot in the center of their forehead.

Keep concentrating. Eventually, you will see the background directly behind the individual becoming brighter and more in focus than the backdrop actually behind them. This is their aura as you see it. It will become clearer the more you focus. You may see several colors or just one or two at first.

To see your own aura, stand or sit in front of a large mirror and follow the same procedure as above.

Meanings of the Colors of the Aura

Most people have one or two colors that dominate their aura. Ordinarily the brighter and more vivid the aura, the healthier and more spiritually evolved one is. The uniformity of the aura also tells us that the individual is more balanced and less scattered or confused. The appearances of dark or smoky-looking colors have negative and unhealthy overtones. Combinations of colors and flashes of colors must be taken into consideration when analyzing the aura. However, for our purposes I am including the basic colors and their meanings.

Auric Colors

White. When speaking of white, which is the combination of colors, remember we're referring to light, not pigment. White (bright light) will always have a positive vibration. We should strive for bright light, not white the color. People confuse a bright light for the color white! It has been noted that in the hours before death, a person's aura becomes the color white and increases in intensity. In many cultures, the aura upon or before death is illustrated in white, not black.

Red. Represents the physical body. It can indicate force, energy, and stamina. This color can represent a person who is self-centered, materialistic, athletic, or sexual. Deeper shades of red lean toward the negative interpretation, while lighter shades the more positive.

Orange. Thoughtfulness, self-control, and optimism. As the sun can be uplifting, so can people who project this color. An individual with orange in their aura can impart insights to others. Some possible challenges may be: falling in love with people who do not reciprocate, as well as issues of trust.

Yellow. Golden yellow can indicate well-being and deep inner wisdom. If the yellow is flushed, this could mean a person tends to be timid and may be looking to start life all over again in a different manner.

Nevertheless, the positive aspects of basic yellow put a person in a natural flow of things. Such people absorb information easily and essentially enjoy life.

Green. Good listener, focusing on healing the self and others. This is the color of various types of healers. Green is nature's color, providing peace and harmony. Someone helpful but not domineering. If you see green leaning toward yellow, it can imply deceit and indecisiveness.

Blue. The color of the spirit, meditation, and truth. All shades of blue are good. Artistic people are apt to have blue in their auras. Sometimes they may be a bit melancholy but for the most part are spiritually minded and dedicated to a cause or project. Blue also can indicate a general healing.

Purple. The most mystical of all the colors. Spirituality, intuitive nature, and seekers. This color does not usually linger and is not too strong for any length of time. Often, it will settle into a deep shade of blue. But when you do see it, it signifies that the person it surrounds has spiritual thoughts and strong insights at the time.

Black. Black has both good and bad qualities and can be very confusing: The *negative side* of black is that it can be a color of a destructive nature. This may indicate evil, cruelty, hatred, depression, and desperately deteriorating health. The *positive side* of black is that it can mean protection! Someone in a very fearful situation may reveal a black aura to protect themselves—just as certain animals such as skunks will excrete an offensive odor, while a different type of animal may turn an altered color or make a threatening noise to protect itself. This is not the constant nature of the animal, but when in fear, it will display these capabilities.

Now that you have a basic idea of how to detect auras in others and yourself, you can see why the aura is so important in regards to psychic protection.

Check your aura in a mirror once a week and work on what may be weakening your energy field. For example, if you find you are seeing a lot more red in your aura than usual, you may be angry with a person, situation, or yourself. Try to work out that anger or the concern that is causing it.

If you have an overwhelming amount of blue, make sure you are not focusing too much on a project and ignoring other issues or situations that need attention.

When the color gray starts to enter your auric scope, pay attention to your health, mood, and eating habits. A healthy aura is like wearing the cosmic armor of resistance.

Why put stress on yourself if there is no need for it? Developing auric sight can save you from much unwanted forms of attack. The auras of other people can unknowingly affect us if we do not protect ourselves. Someone can emanate so much negativity from their aura that we begin to absorb it, if we do not protect ourselves with one or more of the defense methods I offer in the forthcoming pages. However, if you have a friend who has a weak aura, it is best to help him or her heal their aura.

To heal your aura or to help someone else heal theirs, you must do an "auric cleansing." There are several methods of auric cleansing that one may use. Just like in any other form of alternative medicine, there are professionals who perform auric cleansing. This can be done through a professional Reiki practitioner. Reiki means universal life-force energy. Reiki is a method of channeling energy to someone with the intention of healing. A treatment consists of a trained practitioner placing their hands on the client's body or keeping their hands above the body making no physical contact. The practitioner directs the flow of energy and unblocks areas that need attention.

Auric cleansing can energize and clear blockage that may restrict the flow of the life-force energy. Once this is cleared, it may help with depression, fear, low self-esteem, psychical illness, and anything else that may weaken your aura. It is like an energy boost. It raises the vibratory level of your auric field that will break down negative blockage. With knowledge and study, we can also perform Reiki treatments on ourselves.

Bio-Etheric Healing is another form of healing the aura. Trudy Lanitis comments in her book, *Bio-Etheric Healing* (New Falcon Publications), that "Bio-Etheric Healing is an innovative method of alternative healing which uses a set of Communication Skills based on thought processes to direct our Etheric Body, and through it, our full energy field (our Aura) to help in healing work."

It is possible to have this communication directly with one's own energy field. This involves communicating with your etheric body, which is our second nonphysical body.

Basically, one puts oneself into an altered state of consciousness and tells one's bodies one's concerns and listens mentally to a response that is symbolic or in the form of a mental message.

There are also many other energy-healing techniques, such as the use of magnets, healing oils and herbs, crystals and gemstones, as well as many other powerful methods, that can also cleanse the aura. As this area is vast, I will not go into detail about each individual technique. However, I have included one simple but remarkably successful way to cleanse your own aura by use of visualization and intention. With a few modifications you can also use this method to cleanse the aura of someone else whether they are present or not.

How to Heal Your Aura

First determine if your aura is in need of repair. From the previous two sections on seeing auras and the meanings of their colors, you should be able to make this decision by the colors you are seeing, the size of your aura, and the radiance. Nevertheless, if your aura looks excellent but you still feel "out of sorts," I would go ahead with this procedure anyway. Preventative maintenance of your auric field can only be positive.

- Find a time and a place where nothing will disturb you.

- Sit in a chair in the middle of a room.

- Keep your feet flat on the ground.

- If the chair has arms, rest your arms on them with your palms up (in a receiving position). If the chair has no arms, just hold your arms in front of you or rest them on your knees or whatever is comfortable using the same receiving hand placement. *The important factor is that you do not cross your legs, ankles, hands, or arms. This will block the flow of energy. Lying on a bed or floor is also an option.*

- Once you are in position, close your eyes and count up very slowly from one to eight. Eight is a number of power and this seems to be more successful than one through ten.

- As you count up from one to eight, see your body filling with a healing green or blue light. Green is the basic color of healing but blue also has its healing properties. Blue is a color of peace and has a calming effect. You must be the judge of whether green or blue feels better to you. There is no one system of color interpretation that suits everyone. Your intuition will know what is best for you.

- Once you have chosen which color you will use to heal your aura, you can begin.

- See the color entering your toes, going through your ankles, up your legs, past your hips, across your chest, along your shoulders and arms, through your neck, and to the very top of your head. You are now filled with this cleansing and healing light. Feel your body relaxing and being soaked in this purification of light and energy.

- When you feel you are ready, reverse the process and expel the blue or green light. Keeping your eyes closed, see the light now carrying any negativity from your body.

- Count from eight down to one starting at the top of your head. As you count down, see the blue light leaving your body and white light replacing it.

  When you get to your toes, all the blue or green light should be gone. Open your eyes and shake your feet to release any last remaining particles of negativity. You may also shake your hands as well.

- Say to yourself or out loud "My aura is cleansed."

  Cleanse your aura as often as you like or whenever you feel it is necessary.

To cleanse the aura of someone who is not present, sit in a chair as above but visualize this process happening to him or her. Once completed, shake your hands free of their energy and say, "Your aura is cleansed."

The cleansing of the aura will allow you to strengthen it using the white light techniques in this book. You must always start with a clean slate in order to "power up."

Remember, reading the aura of others can enable you to see anger, self-pity, and obsessive behavior before it permeates you. Cleansing the aura provides you with the first building block to fight off the interference of those who may try to bombard you with their own complications and burdens. It is the first stepping-stone to sheltering yourself from the dangers all around you.

PART I

Living Dangers

CHAPTER 1

Energy Vampires

"Just talking to her, I felt drained." I am sure you have uttered those words before. What you may not recognize is that this is not just a sentence to describe the sudden feeling of weariness but the literal truth of the matter! People can inadvertently pierce our protective energy field or aura and empty our energy source. Usually, most do not realize they are taking this action. Nevertheless, someone who holds ill intentions can do this maliciously. People's words or action without words can tax us to the point of consumption!

Individuals we come in contact with in our everyday life such as teachers, salespeople, family members, and friends all have this ability. In fact, you may even be imposing this energy drain onto others. These people are referred to as "Energy Vampires."

The nonliving also have the ability to drain us. But for our purposes, I prefer to associate this expression with the living, as I appoint an alternative name to those on a different plane, which you will read about in Part II.

"Energy Vampires" are not just friends and family who exhaust us with their problems and obsessive behavior. Strangers can also consume that strength from within us in minutes.

There are two different types of Energy Vampires: the Unknowing Energy Vampire and the Malicious Energy Vampire. The Malicious Energy Vampire sets out to deliberately hurt you mentally, physically, spiritually, or all three. These people show no signs of physical aggression but use their minds to attack their prey. This may be an individual who is just evil and enjoys inflicting anguish or pain on others for the mere sport of it!

It can be someone suffering the wrath of divorce or a disagreeable breakup that has produced so much hatred in them for the other person that they sincerely desire to see their ex-partner suffer.

The Malicious Energy Vampire is also found in cases of physical violation or injury. The victim can become so obsessed with revenge or vindictiveness that the victim becomes the attacker by use of their forceful thoughts.

Anyone holding hate and bitterness for another human being, wishing them ill or bad luck, making no attempt to cease such thoughts, is a Malicious Energy Vampire. It is one thing not to like a person but another to wish them harm and desire to see them suffer.

The Unknowing Energy Vampire has a stronger mind than they may realize. In a sense we are all at one time or another Unknowing Energy Vampires. These are people who intrude upon us continually with severe problems and stories of woe. They often act as martyrs and have the "poor me" approach to life.

They also can be someone who visualizes contrary things happening to a person, but deep down does not want anyone to really undergo hardship or anguish. Individuals that fit the Unknowing Energy Vampire category can be bosses, parents, or anyone with authority over another who is too demanding and brings stress on to someone else.

Individuals with tempers are another form of Unknowing Energy Vampires. They use anger to control, although they are aware that harsh words can be upsetting. Their motives may not be to psychically hurt you and they may even claim they just react to a situation and need to vent. Nevertheless, *they* may feel relieved after all is said and done, but *you* are left emotionally barren.

To give you a better understanding of these two categories, here are four examples:

1. The door-to-door magazine salesman is a good example of the Unknowing Energy Vampire. He arrives at the front door and tries to sell you a subscription. You nicely say you already subscribe to that magazine, hoping he will depart. Next he is burrow-

ing in his briefcase for a list of other magazines in which you may have an interest. You tell him no thank you that you just can't afford it. He proceeds to tell you payments can be deferred. You start to slowly close the door, apologizing and saying you have to go now. "How about a friend you may know?" he persists. You finally say, "No . . . sorry," and close the door.

After he has withdrawn, you feel as if you may have won the battle, but he has taken much of your energy troops down with him. This now leaves you with very little backup. He attacked you and transferred some of your energy to himself. Did he do it purposely? It depends. Was he just an ambitious and enthusiastic person? Or did he purposely plan on wearing you down until you surrendered?

Another example of Unknowing Energy Vampires are people who expect you to listen to them recite all of their problems. I am not referring to the occasional problem of a friend, because that's what friends are for. It is the individual who has nothing to say except that which is problematic or self-promoting. No one wants to be around such people. So, as a way of venting, *we* start to discuss these individuals with others and then we in turn become the vampires!

2. The second example of Unknowing Energy Vampires is from my own experience. I travel within two groups of people. Those I will call friends and those I am in contact with for a variety of other reasons, which I refer to as acquaintances (the Unknowing Energy Vampires).

My friends come to visit, share information about their lives, their ups and downs, and then ask politely about me and what is going on in my life. Or upon seeing them, I will immediately inquire as to new events or situations pertaining to their lives. In this manner there is no drain either way and the energy is balanced.

The other group, my acquaintances, pay visits and immediately start talking about themselves, their attainments and calamities, and don't stop until they leave. I could have won the lottery or saved a thousand people from a burning building and they would never know it.

At one point, I was with this second group when an extra person not part of their crowd was present. When she asked about me and I started to speak, I was immediately interrupted and the conversation was at once changed to discussing children. I have no children and am convinced this subject was chosen to purposely make me feel uncomfortable and for these people to take back control of the floor.

Unknowing Energy Vampires don't like to inquire about anyone else as they are in fear you may be doing something or have accomplished something beyond them. They don't want to hear anything good about any other person. Therefore, they become giant vacuum cleaners as they expound about themselves.

This can be exhausting and burdensome. It is as though they are taking all the air out of the room and leaving you none. This will leave the energy in the space unbalanced, causing a deficiency.

3. The Unknowing Energy Vampire can also sometimes exhibit profound strength as in this next case concerning a personal friend of mine. This is an incident were I was also involved but the circumstances surprisingly took on a different twist by the time all was settled. My dear friend is a beautiful young woman married to a wealthy man almost twenty years her senior. When they are with a certain group of her husband's friends, she gets little attention.

The women do not include her in conversation, as they are jealous and the men are afraid to talk to her as the women will not take it well. People assume because of her good looks, she must not be interesting or have anything to say. Not all women are like this, but within this particular group, if they had taken the time to speak with her, they would have discovered that she was not only beautiful but intelligent and interesting as well!

I was in the presence of this group on one occasion and purposely, to see the reaction, I turned to my friend and asked if her clientele had increased in the last year. "Oh, yes it certainly has," she answered. "What do you do?" someone finally blurted out. "I'm a psychologist," she said confidently. "We didn't know that," one grumbled. "Why didn't you tell us?" someone asked her husband.

"I assumed you already knew after the countless times we have all been together," he answered. They looked back and forth at each other and were almost speechless. They concluded that she was an entirely different person than she seemed, because they never took the time to know her or inquire about her life.

After that, the entire mood of the room changed and they were the ones who felt depleted. Every ounce of energy they took from her through time came back to her threefold. It's as though the group lost its strength. Ever since, it is no longer a dilemma for her to be in their presence.

I was quite baffled why she did not resolve this problem a long time ago. Her reply was that she was curious to see how long these people would persist without including her in their conversations. She remarked that she had never seen such selfish people and somewhat wanted to study them. What she didn't realize was that, with a certain amount of ill intention, she was setting them up for a counterstrike! She obviously did not care for this group but allowed them to attack her time and time again.

Now that she had taken them by surprise and become the Energy Vampire herself, she may have gone too far. She started obsessing about these people to herself, telling no one.

She would imagine predicaments where they would be in uncomfortable situations. For instance, when they would mention they were all going boating together, she would see one falling off the dock or the engine failing and the group having to be towed back. The moment she started to picture these images, she would stop, as she did not want to have such thoughts. However, almost daily she would think ill things of them. She would not picture anything totally hateful but rather things that would annoy or embarrass them.

As the days went on and she tried to stop these images, she heard that one of the six people had become very ill. She was not pleased to hear that, but did not think much of it, as people do get sick on occasion. A week later she heard that one of these individuals had a sudden diagnosis that eventually led to surgery. Within two months every single one of the group was ailing from a serious affliction. The first one that became sick was the one she liked the least, and the last one was the one she liked the most.

When telling me this story, she was upset and felt she had projected so much negativity on these people that she had contributed to their illnesses. Just as I feel the power of prayer can aid in healing, I also feel the opposite can make people physically ill. I recommended every night she pray for these people to the God of her understanding or higher power. She prayed faithfully, and slowly every single one recovered. You be the judge as to whether you think she abated the disease and afflictions.

The mind is very powerful and so is the energy that we can transmit. Was this just coincidence?

Visualization can be an enormously powerful tool. It can be used for good or in a harmful way. Obviously by sharing this story I have given you an obscure road map of how to impair someone with thought and intention. This was not my aim. But how can you defend yourself if you do not understand how the weapons of your enemies work? My friend imposed a surprise attack when they were not prepared.

4. I feel very strongly about being taken off guard, as I directly fell victim to a strange and unwarranted attack in Mexico. This, my fourth example, is a perfect instance of the Malicious Energy Vampire. Some years ago I was traveling through Mexico in a truck with my friend and magazine photographer, David Stahl. We were there to take photographs and also purchase pre-Columbian reproductions for resale in a small import business we owned.

The two of us traveled through desert and mountains. The weather was 73 degrees, the sky sunny, and all seemed well. We drove and talked and laughed and tried to understand the words on the Mexican radio station. I felt very free and happy to be alive as I was encountering a different part of the world. The last thing in my consciousness was to protect myself with a psychic shield in case someone would try to attack me with his or her mind!

About three o' clock in the afternoon we pulled onto a dirt road that took us to a small Mexican town, one I am sure was not on any map. There was a fountain in the middle of town and vendors all around with their colorful blankets that lay on the ground filled with crafts and other items for sale. There was a religious ceremony going on in honor of one of the saints.

The people were smiling, there was music in the streets, food was being cooked, and children were playing. A happy town, from what I could see. Upon pulling in, David was very cautious, as we all should be traveling abroad to remote areas. However, he had real concern on his face and this troubled me. I asked him what was wrong. David replied there was nothing wrong that he could see, but he had a "funny feeling."

Just about at that moment a small boy with dark hair came running up to our truck. *"Hola, hola,"* he shouted. It was as if he had been waiting for us. We asked him in Spanish if he knew of any stores or places where we might purchase some pre-Columbian re-productions of Aztec and Mayan gods. "*Sí,* follow me," he said joy-ously.

We followed in the truck slowly behind him as he walked to a very isolated road. From there we could drive no farther and had to walk. Most people probably would not have even gone with this young boy as the feeling immediately started to change when we got out of the truck. However, David and I, being adventurous, continued on. We were on a mission to find these statues and we kept our minds set on the goal!

We sauntered through a long sandy and pebbled path. We walked over holes and the foliage on either side started to get big-ger and arched over us until we were in a tunnel of trees, where light was barely seen on such a sunny day. We eventually came to a ridge and had to descend about eight feet. As we walked down the mound of dirt, I heard the squawk of a bird. To my left was a hawk sitting on a perch with a chain of some type around its leg. The sight of this bird made be feel very out of sorts.

As we proceeded, I noticed that the smiling little boy started to change his demeanor. He suddenly seemed as if he was in an al-tered state, somewhat dazed or mesmerized. At the bottom of the mound was a shed that was half buried in the ground. As we entered through an old wooden door, walls of black mud surrounded us.

If Hollywood wanted to create anything resembling a witch's den, they could not have done a better job! And for the record, any-one who is Wiccan or practices white witchcraft, I am by no means associating the two. I know the Wiccan creed is, "Do as you will but hurt no one," and I have never met a Wiccan I didn't like. But this was not Wicca! It was black magic occultism without a doubt.

The unseen influences in this place were overwhelming. You did not have to be psychic to feel the oppression and malaise of these surroundings.

On the tables were herbs, feathers, string, molcahetes (chili grinders), and a few things I could not identify or attempt to put a name to. I understand and recognize the value of natural herbs for the use of healing and protection, but I sensed these were grown and processed for corrupt application. Similarly, certain medica-tions may help us, but put into the wrong hands, they can be used to hurt us or to bring on addiction.

As I started to look more intensely, I noticed this place had no electricity or water. There were candles that gave off diffused light. I could see chickens and roosters through a back door that was opened but five steps up.

There were shelves on the back walls primitively attached to the mud and clay. Set on the shelves were pre-Columbian reproductions of figures that were obviously handmade and baked in the sun as opposed to being fired in a kiln. These figures were all very phallic and without a doubt male! There were about fifty and they were all desperately sinister-looking.

Suddenly I noticed the little boy was gone, and David and I were alone in this hollow. It appeared as though it were midnight. We looked at each other and did not say a word. We sensed it was not a good time to talk, as we felt someone would be listening.

Under normal circumstances I would have picked up one of the idols and examined it. Nevertheless, I did not want to touch them as I feel handmade objects can become impregnated with emanations of the person who created them.

You might imagine the thoughts that went through our minds! We were two Americans originally staying in San Miguel de Allende who had ventured away with no one knowing where we were, no cell phones, had followed a little boy who seemed to vanish, and we had walked literally into a remote hole in the ground far away from town! To say the least, we felt like leaving.

As we started to turn and head for the door, since no one seemed to be there, we saw an old woman starting to descend from the back door down into the den. She was very elderly and hunched over. She was thin and her skin was wrinkled. This woman had long black hair with streaks of gray, which was severely disheveled. As she shuffled slowly toward us in old sandals, she clutched her black sweater, which was hanging loosely over an old gray dress. I felt as if I were in a Halloween film. Regardless, we tried not to act startled and wore our best smiles.

As David and I were used to traveling through poor towns in Mexico, we never wore expensive-looking clothing or jewelry. We tried to blend in and stuck to basic jeans and sweatshirts so as not to come off as saucy Americans. We combined our casual clothing with our smiles, so for all intents and purposes, I do not believe we looked threatening. David asked her in broken Spanish if she had any more statues.

With a shaking hand, she reached to a shelf for one of the idols.

She started to hand it to David. He responded in a friendly manner explaining that those were very nice, but he was looking for something a bit different. She just nodded her head and pointed to the display. Under a more conducive atmosphere and just to be polite, we would have bought something and left. But we did not want to have those figures in our possession.

I felt that, by merely picking one up, the vibration could have possibly rubbed off on me. It was as if David and I telepathically made an agreement not to come in contact with those images.

Suddenly, she turned her gaze to me. And what a gaze it was! The Egyptians and other cultures referred to "the evil eye" and now I know what they meant. It is a gaze from an individual who has ill intentions toward you. In fact, that is one reason the Egyptians wore blue eye shadow ... to ward off the "evil eye."

As I was not wearing blue eye shadow and at the time psychic protection from the likes of someone like her was beyond me, I just kept smiling and nodding.

In retrospect, I feel she must have sensed I was an intuitive and deemed she would show me a thing or two about who really had abilities!

Well, I am not so vain or egotistical to tell you who won. She did. I was rendered defenseless from her psychic aggression. David was a bit on edge, but seemed okay.

We finally left and wanted to run out but walked at a normal pace as not to insult her. As we walked down the pathway back to the truck, we were both fearful she would send someone after us.

As we arrived at the truck, I suddenly started to feel nauseous. I put it off to just being upset at the surroundings of her home. As we drove, I became dizzy to the point of almost fainting. I asked David to finally stop the truck, as I had never felt so ill in my life. I was sweating, nauseous, and light-headed.

This had at no time ever happened to me! I was sure that the food was not tainted as the food we ate that morning in San Miguel was food I had cooked myself and was totally fresh. David was fine and felt no physical problems.

We finally made it back after hours of traveling. I was hunched over the entire driving time in agony. That is the only time in my life I actually thought death looked more promising than what I was feeling.

I took a shower holding on to the walls to maintain my balance, in order to get the energy of that place and woman off me. I sat on the floor of the shower to wash my hair, as I could not stand without hands braced on something.

I scrubbed my hair intensely, and as I washed, using the water as a form of purification, I visualized whatever she had inflicted on me vanishing down the drain.

I buried the clothes I had on, as if permeated by a skunk, for I never wanted to wear them again. Then I said, "With the God of my understanding and the power of all things, bring me back to awareness and make me strong again."

I sat and stared at the fire in the fireplace for a few minutes and I was well once more. I professed I would never allow that to happen again.

This evidently was a psychic attack with the intention to harm. It was this situation that inspired and led me to create a way of protection for such unusual occurrences.

CHAPTER 2

Dysfunctional Relationships

S top! You're giving my psyche a hernia! How much baggage can it carry? Any relationship, be it romantic or a friendship, can bombard us with energies we don't want, need, or benefit from. So why do we allow activity in our lives that weighs us down and depresses us? Why do the moods and conduct of others affect us? How many times have you heard someone say, "I am in a very dysfunctional relationship"?

It has become so common that I really believe it is almost becoming the chic or trendy way to live. Why don't people just dissolve that negative energy and move on? A lot of questions . . . but really some simple answers.

It has been my experience that when people have been in dysfunctional relationships for a long period of time, they are so drained of energy, they don't have the forcefulness to heal their auric field and tend to their own needs. Not even a glimpse of a protective shield is left standing around them. They are totally exposed and don't even know it.

People who are so accustomed to dealing with conflicting individuals absorb others' negativity like a sponge. When the sponge starts to dry out, they latch on to someone who will once again saturate them with a river of "bad vibes." Hence, one can go from one bad relationship to another. Sometimes we will recognize that we have to start looking for different types of people to associate with. However, even though that is moving in the right direction, we can still suffer from negative vibrations hovering around us. We must literally "clear the air."

Here's an example. After many years of relationships with men that never worked out, Joyce, a businesswoman from New York, found a wonderful man she eventually married. He was quite a catch—always happy, and constantly seeing the good in all situations. He projected love and happiness to all who came his way. If he was ever down, he dealt with it and never complained. Life was good and Joyce decided she needed some female friends. However, Joyce ended up surrounding herself with female friends who had nothing but pessimism in their lives, were constantly complaining, and believed their destiny was to be unhappy.

Joyce, being intelligent and now starting to feel devoid of strength, sought counseling from a respected psychologist in the New York area. She was told she needed to remove herself from individuals who were too much of a drain on her. Her comfort zone was in the form of being a victim and a martyr.

Taking this advice, Joyce removed herself from her friends. In a very nice manner, she explained that her new husband and job were very time consuming. She explained she could no longer devote as much time or participation to friends as she used to. As a result, Joyce hardly heard from her friends again. They all understood and did not wish her anything but happiness.

Nevertheless, why was Joyce still feeling depressed? She was no longer exhausted by her needy friends, she was married to a man who was upbeat, her job was good, money was flowing, and her health was in order. With her psychologist, she worked through trauma and childhood issues that could have been a cause. But she still felt downhearted. Chemicals or medication to lift her spirit were not the answer, either!

After talking to Joyce about her despair, I realized she was under psychic attack. But from whom, Joyce wanted to know? She had no enemies, she basically liked herself, and there was no negativity around her.

That is what she did not understand. Psychic attack can come from people miles away who are doing it unconsciously.

After encouraging Joyce to make a few phone calls to her old friends, we discovered that although they were no longer in her life, they used to think about her every time they became troubled.

"What would Joyce say or do if she knew I was feeling like this?" one friend thought.

Another friend said, when she would often cry about the problems in her life, she would also think of calling Joyce but would always decide not to bother her. Joyce was under psychic bombardment and didn't have a clue! The thoughts of these ladies were traveling to her at light speed. She had become so sensitive to her friends' feelings and emergencies that she could pick up their impact from anywhere. Just as a mother can intuitively tell when a child is in trouble, she was absorbing all the woe and agony from her old friends.

Joyce learned some basic daily forms of protection (which you will learn later in the book). Ever since, she has not had any unusual bouts of anguish and dismay. She can now deflect negative thought-forms that whirl around her.

Another case involved a couple, Gail and Joe. Gail was a middle-aged registered nurse and Joe was her live-in boyfriend. Joe used to call himself a "free spirit." This translated to mean: a good-natured guy, attractive, did not want responsibility, lazy, didn't want to work, and looked for "get rich quick" schemes. He kept busy, and to talk to him, you would think he was right around the corner from hitting it big in some type of venture. Although Joe would clean the house, do laundry, and even make dinner, Gail didn't need a maid; she needed someone to help her pay the bills!

Yet again, he was faithful, her friends loved him, and she pretended for appearances' sake that he made much more money than he did.

Gail was getting weary of working so hard, and as the years rolled by, she needed some type of help to support them in the lifestyle they were living. When confronting Joe about this and suggesting he find employment, he had a better idea. Why not just scale down and live somewhere less expensive? He kept insisting that he needed to spend his time developing a new idea he had about keeping mosquitoes away from picnic tables!

Gail once again gave him the benefit of the doubt and thought that perhaps she was with a genius on the brink of success. Everything had to be invented somewhere. Perhaps Joe could be the one.

Gail worked overtime at the hospital and began to get very fatigued. She no longer had her former enthusiasm when she saw Joe. She also noticed the meals he made didn't taste as good as before.

Joe, too, was losing his eagerness to help. The laundry now sat for days and the house was not as tidy as he used to keep it. Were they falling out of lust or love? Obviously they were, but they were also attacking each other on the astral battlefield. Joe used to visualize what it would be like to be with a different woman. Perhaps someone so financially secure she did not have to work. That way she would have more time to spend with him, supporting and helping him launch his projects. He felt Gail fell short. He started giving out feelings of resentment toward her.

Gail used to envision what it would be like to go back to working just one shift or having a man in her life who would carry his own weight. She, in turn, was sending strong signals to Joe!

As Gail was in the medical profession, she knew many health professionals and made an appointment with a relationship counselor with whom they both felt comfortable.

Naturally, Joe was told to get a job, and Gail was told she had allowed the situation by letting it go on too long. The two came to a compromise. Joe got a part-time job so Gail could stop working overtime. That way he could pursue his inventions and Gail pitched in with household duties. A win-win situation, right?

For a few months, things were going smoothly. Joe was working for the Forest Bureau and Gail felt the financial burden was not totally on her. Suddenly Gail just asked Joe to leave. As she said, "Something in my heart just couldn't stand to be with him any longer." She did not ponder the thought, talk about it to friends, or obsess about it for days. She just wanted him out! He did not do anything to warrant such behavior and he had thought everything was going well.

After Joe had been gone for months, she tried to look back at what had made her snap. He was doing more than when they'd first met. He had actually improved. She felt she was not acting like a caretaker or wanting to mother him. Gail was not afraid he may enjoy working and someday leave her. So what was it?

Gail said she felt a terrible force she could no longer fight that provoked her to break all ties to him. Who was it? What was it?

It was Joe. He had more resentment and frustration than he let on. Although he knew he was doing the right thing, he still resented the fact that he had to work. Unintentionally, he was chipping away at the protective covering she had kept in place for so long. That covering that kept her body, mind, and sprit in balance. Once he had started to show more promise in all areas of life, she backed off and let her shield weaken. Consequently, it became brittle and just suddenly shattered one day and she lashed out.

It was Joe's own thoughts and negativity that broke Gail down. His mind was far more powerful than he had imagined. The fact that he never talked to anyone about his bitterness and kept it to himself made it even stronger as it was not dissipated by conversation or communication.

Joe and Gail went their separate ways. The war was over and nobody won. Energy meeting energy . . . it was a stalemate.

When two people are together in a partnership of any kind, they both need to protect themselves from the other's energy. One should allow a certain amount of energy to come in, but be aware of what vibrations are needed to be kept out.

To accomplish this, I suggest using what I refer to as a *psychic strainer*. You can't buy one or construct one. But you can use it to separate clear love and reliable integrity from the pulp of instability and anxiety.

Creating a Psychic Strainer: A Form of Protection

When you first meet someone for whom you feel a strong attraction, pay close attention. Since they attract you on some level, you must not be smitten and forget to defend yourself.

The best way for me to describe how to use this technique is to visualize what might look like cheesecloth, the size of a door, hanging in front of you. This should be applied at the onset of a conversation with your potential partner. It protects yet allows energy in and out.

If you create a solid shield that nothing can penetrate, you may appear as a cold person who is stern and defensive. This way you can be cautious, yet leave yourself a bit open and somewhat accessible. This will allow some of your true feelings to shine through without giving yourself totally away.

Engage in normal conversation, using no "trick questions" or scenarios in order to decide whether a person has a psychological disorder. Determine what kind of person you think this individual may be.

Sometimes the universe gives us the simplest and most obvious clues, but we disregard them. Trust your intuition. You may accept or dispel this individual's energy.

Putting up a "psychic strainer" should assist you in being more aware of what is being said. For instance, in your first conversation, perhaps someone mentions his cable TV is getting too expensive. He continues saying he would rather not have a television if costs keep escalating.

Later, you learn he is financially well-to-do with a high-paying job. That person may be just "cheap"! Was he joking or being serious?

If you can deal with people of this nature and feel the same way, you may have a good match. However, if this bothers you, add to your psychic strainer by including another layer of white light and exercise a bit more caution.

Don't be taken in by only a nice smile and a good build. In the long run it may be the things you first saw as a positive at your initial meeting that might be your demise.

Every time you find an area where you are not like-minded, add another layer to that shield. If by the end of the first hour you have so many layers in front of you that symbolically you cannot see, this may not be the person for you.

No one is perfect, but it is those imperfections that make us all unique. Nevertheless, there are certain things that are important to us, and if you don't see those qualities within the first few weeks, I would reconsider.

So many people hope someone will change or assume their potential partner is just going through tough times. Although this may well be the case, do not let your guard down.

I believe from my experience dealing with the depletion of energy and practicing psychic self-defense, that when someone thinks they are in love, they let their psychic buffers completely down. Then, they may end up getting hurt, feeling foolish, and being used. Before they realize it, they cannot retrieve their vital forces, unless they completely remove themselves from the other person's energy.

Remember, sometimes the thing we like most about someone

from the beginning is the very thing that causes us to break up with him or her in the end. I offer you three examples:

First day you meet . . . "He was the cutest guy at the party, he's not real intelligent, but he hasn't had the opportunities I have."

Six months later . . . "I can never trust him with all those women chasing after him. Not to mention, I can't use 'big words' around him or he thinks I am showing off my education. What's his problem?"

First day . . . "She is very frugal and practical, not a high maintenance woman. She'll never try to use me when it comes to money!"

Six months later . . . "It's none of her business if I buy a motorcycle. It's not her money. She thinks I spend too much money on my clothes too! What's gotten into her lately?"

First day . . . "I love the way she knows so much about astrology and meditation and is a such a good vegetarian cook. She is very different and interesting. I can learn a lot from her and probably be healthier too. She is not like anyone else I've ever met. I love a woman who is unusual and full of surprises."

Three weeks later . . . "I just want a burger and to go to see a movie. Who cares what my aura is doing or not doing? I'm embarrassed to take her to restaurants out of fear she will ask the waitress if the spoon used to scoop meatballs is the same spoon used to ladle the plain pasta! She's too weird for me!"

Sometimes we are in doubt as to whether we actually are interested in someone and whether they are interested in us. A good way to tell is to use a method I call a *pulsating white light*. This is a way to pick up the other person's frequency.

In a quiet comfortable area, sit in a chair or anyplace comfortable for you. Close your eyes and visualize a white light around your intended's entire body. It may look like a cloud or a balloon. You may just see it appear or may want to observe it travel from the toes to above their head. (This is a very basic way to protect someone with white light and you will read more about it later.) This protects that individual from any negativity that you may unwillingly send their way. Next, visualize a second white light that forms an upside down V emanating from above their head to the bridge of their nose. It may look similar to a big pointed hat. Imagine it slowly pulsating with little surges of light.

Now, focus on the individual's third eye (the center of their forehead). Notice if their face becomes clearer, brighter, and happier or more blurred and dimmer. If it is brighter, there may be a positive flow of forces emanating from the two of you. If it is dimmer, the energies are probably not conducive. Be honest with yourself. What do you see and feel?

Perhaps you may perceive that you are purposely making the light appear brighter and clearer, as you *want* to continue in the direction of a relationship. Be as honest as possible, yet do not overconcern yourself with whether you are really seeing the light brighter or not. I believe the subconscious will find itself one way or the other.

The reality of it is, two frequencies that are harmonic will find their way to each other. If you see this person as a glowing, happy frequency, tune into it as they most likely feel the same from you. If you do not pick up a clearer and more vivid picture, reconsider your position with this newfound soul.

CHAPTER 3

Careers That Are Prone to Psychic Attack

Certain professions, by virtue of what they are, open themselves to psychic assault. Although this energy invasion emanates from other people, it is not the same as Energy Vampires.

Medical, legal, and financial professionals; law enforcement personnel; airline and sales representatives; as well as negotiators in the creative arts are the hardest hit by psychic assault. They all basically suffer from the same dilemma. They can become *psychic sponges*, absorbing the negativity from an individual before that person ever comes in contact with them.

Healthcare Professionals

These individuals are dealing with pain, discomfort, and imbalance. One minute they experience joy that someone has recovered and the next they are inundated by fear and heartbreak from another patient's concerned friends and relatives.

Health care is an admirable field whether you choose to be a doctor, nurse, caregiver, or holistic/spiritual healer. Anyone who is dedicated to keeping us sound must be commended. Unfortunately, due to the fear affiliated with these services, men and women in this profession are under psychic attack the moment they arrive at their workplace.

An emergency room attendant is a good example of someone who is totally besieged. Almost all their senses are being constantly bombarded from the moment they meet the patient.

Sight.   Blood, lacerations, and broken bones are only a few of the disturbing things they look at daily.

Hearing.   The distraught voices of people in pain are all a part of a day's work.

Smell.   Vital fluids, chemicals, and antiseptics are being inhaled regularly.

Touch.   Unwillingly, the mere touch of a patient from the healthcare professional may impose pain to the sufferer.

Usually, these devoted healers are prepared for what is to come daily and realize this is part of the career they chose. Some will feel they may have become immune to it. That may be true for a while, but I feel if they do not shield themselves daily with some type of defense mechanism, all this sorrow and suffering can eventually penetrate their psyches and their physical bodies, leaving them consumed and sometimes even physically ill. Healthcare professionals should keep eucalyptus or the aroma of eucalyptus in their home as it relieves stress.

Dentists are another group of healthcare professionals who are under more duress than most. The idea of going to the dentist to some people is painful in itself. How can we have happy feelings for a person who will soon be inflicting pain on us and then have to pay him or her to do it? Unintentionally, your dentist can make you feel guilty by asking questions such as, "Have you been flossing lately?" Their conversation is about bleeding gums, tooth decay, root canals, and tooth loss, which is not conducive to a positive relationship!

I believe a dentist can feel the vibrations of a client days before the client walks through the door. Someone could be obsessing about the pain he or she believes the dentist will administer. Hence, the dentist will start to absorb that energy long before the appointment. This could be the reason dentists are said to have one of the highest suicide rates in the country.

I recommend dentists should place a small, inconspicuous container or pouch holding the five gemstones I have listed below, hidden in a plant container or even under a sofa. These stones will promote the properties they carry. If they are displayed outwardly, people may tend to examine them and give them too many foreign energies, which would deplete the stones of their potency.

Chrysolite: Supports emotional balance.
Fluorite: Like fluoride, will benefit the teeth and bones. Stabilizing and calming properties.
Jet: Reduces stress. Relieves depression.
Lapis lazuli: Boosts the immune system.
Pink coral: Soothing and can resolve conflicts.

Airline Professionals

This profession has a similar predicament. Upon making a mere reservation to take flight, someone fearful of flying begins to emit that energy to all involved. Pilots, flight attendants, and reservationists are constantly combating psychic aggression. Picture the surge of fear a pilot consumes from the passengers as they leave the ground, as well as when they land.

Airline professionals should have in their possession a piece of petrified wood or a tiger's-eye gemstone. *Passengers with a fear of flying would do well to carry the same.* It protects and will balance you. These items are grounding and representative of the earth, which is far from you while you are soaring through the clouds.

Law Enforcement

They can put us in jail, give us our freedom, impair our lives, or keep us safe. People love and hate them, depending on what side of the scale you are on at any given moment.

They are exhausted by the contradiction of the positive and negative thought-forms that gust upon them like an unforeseen storm. They have trouble keeping their scales balanced. A police officer may one day save a life and the next day get shot. These lively professionals are usually energetic and can have a natural toughness that takes form as a psychic defense field. They are not even aware they are creating this defense. They often protect themselves without even being aware of what they are doing.

When we are extremely busy, physically moving and thinking, it is difficult for us to fall victim to psychic aggression. This actually goes for any profession that deals with activity.

The police officer who is on a mission is safer from psychic warfare than the officer that is directing traffic. The active officer's mind is spinning like a fan and blows away anything that can break through his energy field.

The inactive officer leaves himself or herself open to particles of negativity that may float his way, as his mind is more still. This is true of other professions, as well, that deal with activity. Sometimes we must recognize that this is a part of their job and what they are retained to do. Law enforcement professionals should carry a piece of bloodstone or wear it in a form of jewelry.

Bloodstone aids in increasing courage and helps in avoiding dangerous situations.

Legal Professionals

Lawyers, legal assistants, accountants, and all those who deal with legal documents are considered to be under more psychic invasion than various other fields. Yes, a lawyer may present you with a lawsuit that you do not take kindly to, resulting in you emitting to him or her thoughts of animosity.

Yet that same attorney may help you get your lottery winnings in order, resulting in your emitting joy, happiness, and tranquillity toward this helpful advocate.

Your accountant may neglect to include enough deductions in your taxes but in another instance save you money. These types of occupations struggle with balancing the daily extremes. If they help us, we like them and regenerate echoes of goodness toward them. If they should present information to us that causes stress or disappointment, we may end up unconciously directing negative vibrations at them, which can weaken their auras. Legal professionals should also pay close attention to the phases of the moon.

It is not recommended that legal contracts of any kind be signed three days before, on, or after a full moon. The vibrations of the moon's pull can cause chaos and confusion unless you know how to take that powerful vibration and use it to your benefit. Sometimes there is no choice and contracts or agreements can't wait, so before signing, whether during the day or at night, visualize the moon if you cannot actually see it at the time.

Say silently as you sign the document, "I sign this paper with the intent to give it strength and not chaos." If there are other people with you, they need not be aware of what you are doing. If you cannot remember the entire sentence, merely think, "Strength, not chaos."

Salespeople

A salesperson is typically perceived as pushy, aggressive, and often even shady. Why? Because we tend to remember the negative more than the positive. We remember the lady who follows us around the store relentlessly questioning our needs to the point of being intrusive. But we forget the fellow who simply smiles and says if there is anything he can do, he will be nearby and tells you to take your time.

While trying to make a living at what appears to be a harmless job, sales representatives are on the front lines of battle. They are still getting hit after people leave a store or establishment.

We continue to discuss them. "That car salesperson was getting on my nerves. Why don't these people just let us look?" "If I call that realtor, he'll never leave me alone, demanding all sorts of answers about relocation."

Admittedly, often a salesperson can be too aggressive, bringing battle on him or herself. But because their profession demands them to be forthright, we tend to fabricate an aversion before even meeting them. "I don't want to go into that store because I'm afraid that saleslady looking out the window will pounce on me!" You don't know her, have never set eyes on her, but you are assuming she will harass you. You're preparing for war and she doesn't even know there is a conflict. If forty people per day thought in a similar manner, the salesperson would leave work exhausted and not even know why! No one even came into the store!

If the salesperson were to have protected herself with a shield of psychic protection, this negative energy being flung at her from all directions could be dismissed. This way our trusty sales representative would not be depleted by the close of the day.

Salespeople should not display *large* calendars or *large* clocks in their private residences. It focuses on deadlines and quotas, eventually squandering what is left of their psychic zeal and reminding them of the pressure they experience at the workplace.

Creative Arts Representatives

Agents, publishers, managers, editors, and instructors who deal with creative people can very quickly be bereft of their power supply. Yes, these are the professionals who contribute to furthering careers in art, music, acting, writing, and filmmaking. Much love and thanks can travel out to them when things for their clients are going well, but what about all the talent they must refuse? Daily they must reject the "Four P's"—people, proposals, propositions, and projects.

Creative arts delegates are hit full circle, first by disappointed individuals who were counting on their representation as a guiding light to success. Attack comes next when they are negotiating difficult contracts or deals, and finally, when they are not able to convince peers or associates of the value they may see in a person or project.

The intuitive notion that someone or something will be successful when no one else sees the latent talent can be very stressful. The psychic strikes they must undergo could leave them wounded for years. Just when one wound starts to heal, another one is suffered.

These representatives are so overwhelmed, they do not have time to relax. They deal with the egotistical, the temperamental, the flamboyant, the deadlines, "the comedy and the tragedy."

These people might consider placing a *live* aloe vera plant in their office somewhere. It does not have to be large. Perhaps just a small plant that would sit on a shelf or desk. Aloe, known as "the first aid plant," promotes healing and is easily grown indoors.

We need first aid usually when dealing with an unexpected accident such as a burn, cut, or insect bite. So why do people in the creative arts need aloe vera near them? Because everything does not necessarily mean first aid of the physical body. Agents, editors, and managers deal with unexpected incidents daily. Besides being beneficial for heartburn, ulcers, digestion, and much more, aloe vera can promote mental balance just by looking at it. It represents soothing properties, healing effects, growth, hope, and longevity. What a burst of vitality can be obtained by just thinking about those qualities when feeling bewildered!

I have a small garden of aloe vera, and when I am feeling dismayed, I go outside and take a look at my plants. They just make me smile. Seems simple? Sometimes the smallest things in nature can do the greatest things.

Computers and Office Equipment May Drain You—Beware!

A note to all those who use computers and office equipment daily for long periods of time. As I feel these are things we all deal with daily and your health is your greatest asset, I have included this information for your awareness and to propose to you a holistic solution.

Many businesspeople, self-employed proprietors, and even individuals in the creative fields are using computers and other electronic devices. We can hardly ignore them. But extended use of any electronic mechanism can drain our energy!

One morning when feeling fine and well rested, I sat down in the chair in my office. Suddenly, the mere sight of my computer monitor made me tired. There it was, that big square screen that would soon start to assault me the minute I turned on the switch. Like a viper, it would lash out at me and in minutes I would feel weary. I asked a friend of mine his secret for dealing with his daily computer work and he quickly said "magnets." After inquiring how they worked, where to get them, and how they could help restore my energy, he pointed me to Ray T. Jacobs, DVM.

Dr. Jacobs is a veterinarian/author/speaker/teacher. He conducts biomagnetic and herbal workshops and is presently developing new magnetic therapy products. He serves as a consultant to several magnetic manufacturing companies.

His credits for his veterinarian work are immense. He has a traditional and holistic practice for small animals using herbs, homeopathics, magnetic therapy, laser therapy, radionics, and nutritional therapeutic procedures. His knowledge of magnetic therapy is abundant, and because of his advice and expertise, he has helped many people through the use of magnetic therapy.

As I believe in the *law of numbers*, I interviewed many people who had used magnetic therapy to aid them in "computer burnout." I heard a great number of successful testimonies. I would not recommend anything I myself have not tried, so I gave it a chance. After taking Dr. Jacobs's advice, I too have a success story. I was not exhausted by the end of the day. My vision seemed to improve and I no longer disliked sitting at my computer. Why? The use of magnets.

Dr. Jacobs writes, "Radiation may be slowly killing you. For every report that states otherwise, there are ten reports proving your health is at risk."

You cannot hide from EMR (electromagnetic radiation). Everything electrical emits radiation because electromagnetic radiation is caused by the breakdown of current and every appliance operates on this principle. There is even EMR radiating from appliances when they are plugged in but not turned on!

Some people are more affected by some frequencies of electrically emitted electromagnetic radiation than they are by other frequencies. Tolerance levels differ from one person to another.

Our body also has an electromagnetic circuit, and when we come into contact with any extraneous electromagnetic radiation source such as electrical appliances, television, radios, microwave, cordless phones, computer video display units, mobile phones, etc., our body attracts the radiation like a magnet. The electromagnetic radiation causes an overload in our body circuits wherever there is a weak link.

This is the place where ill health manifests. Everyone has weak links; for some it may be the kidneys, while for others it may be the heart, lungs, brain, liver, or some other organ system.

Mobile phone users complain of painful ears and headaches. Mobile phones are dangerous devices that emit microwave radiation.

We carry them on our bodies for hours, and contrary to what people believe, using an earpiece increases the radiation to our head. The wire acts as an antenna for the EMR to travel along to our brain.

An office environment is unhealthy with fax machines, photocopiers, fluorescent lighting, computers, telephones, and electrical cables, just to mention a few sources of EMR. A computer monitor gives off harmful very low frequency pulsating EMR from 15,000 to 240,000 hertz. Very low frequency radiation could be more harmful to your body than radiation from electric power lines.

With the rapid increase in computer technology, it has now become necessary to also protect yourself from the computer's central processing unit (CPU), as well as the video display unit.

Exposure to the radiation from a computer monitor is similar and cumulative. Sooner or later you will exceed your tolerance level and become ill.

Airplanes are at the top of the scale when it comes to radiation. Many people complain of jet lag, when actually it is "electromagnetic radiation lag." There is a difference between how the body reacts to time change and jet lag.

What can be done? How can we protect ourselves from this electromagnetic radiation fiasco? Dr. Jacobs offers a solution that he feels is a step in the right direction. He states, "There are many devices and techniques recommended to protect your body from electromagnetic radiation (EMR), many of which I have experimented with and found most are not of much benefit.

"I use a low-energy *magnetic necklace* to partially protect my body from EMR. As a result, I don't experience headaches, dizziness, drowsiness, lack of energy, clouded thinking, or that wiped-out feeling when I wear magnetic devices while working at my computer! The magnetic energy seems to repel the electromagnetic radiation."

I, too, have taken Dr. Jacobs's advice. I keep a magnetic necklace on a hook on the wall next to my computer. Before turning on my computer, I slip the necklace on and wear it until I am through for the day. Some people wear theirs constantly but I choose to keep it for this sole purpose. Also, when I remove the necklace, it serves as a signal that the workday is completed. When I put the necklace back, I also leave my concerns and tribulations for the day on the hook along with it!

Also, when possible, give yourself a "computer vacation." And that does not mean surfing the Net for discount cruises! Get away from it or use it at a minimum. Restore your vitality. Plan your "vacation" in advance.

Tell yourself you will not use your computer for twenty-four hours on a weekend or give yourself some time frame. If you are someone who must retrieve daily e-mails, do so, but do no more than the minimum.

All working people should carry out regular forms of defense at work and home (see Part V for guidance in daily forms of protection).

CHAPTER 4

Hexes, Spells, and Curses

There are numerous definitions, as well as schools of thought, when it comes to hexes, spells, and curses. Some imply that a hex, a spell, and a curse are one and the same. Although all are connected to the use of magic or the occult, there are differences.

Hex

The word "hex" actually comes from the German word for sorcery, *hexincraft*, and is defined in most dictionaries as "evil curses or spells," showing little variance among the three terms. Research, folklore, and our ancient cultures, however, demonstrate that there are differences.

Herbert B. Greenhouse describes the word "hex" with a bit of a different twist in his well-researched book, *The Book of Psychic Knowledge*. He also demonstrates an apparent difference between a hex, a spell, and a curse.

According to Greenhouse, the "hex" had been used in nearly all cultures, primitive or sophisticated, as a form of black magic. An image of the enemy is molded in wax or other pliable substances, his or her name is scratched on it, then it is pricked with a sharp point or melted over heat while an incantation is uttered. The old-style witch (not Wiccan) claimed she could ruin crops and cause lightning and thunder this way. "Murder by effigy" (representation) was forbidden in Anglo-Saxon law. The reader is urged to refrain from this practice, as the "hex" may turn back on him or her.

Greenhouse describes what we may regard as a voodoo doll or the like. A hex involves a form or an object that represents the intended, whereas technically a spell or a curse does not need such a representation, but sometimes one still may be used in such practices. There are those who feel hexes are made to protect, to draw love, or to symbolize and strengthen a partnership. I put these positive aspects into the category of spells, not hexes.

Curse

A curse is an obtrusive dark magic type of conjuration placed upon a person or people with the intention of causing them harm. This is what is often referred to as black magic. One either lays or throws a curse. You do not cast a curse as you would a spell. A curse can occur immediately after being thrown or sit inactive for years. We have all heard of the curses laid on families, which besiege them year after year and pass on through generations. Not only can a curse be thrown on an individual or family, but it can also be thrown on groups as a form of revenge, or even on our country's leaders.

A good illustration of this is the "Curse of Tecumseh." The Curse of Tecumseh is the "successions of deaths to Presidents in the U.S. elected in years ending in a zero."

After the epic battle of Tippecanoe in 1811, legend has it that a Shawnee Indian Chief named Tecumseh sent General William Henry Harrison a message prophesying that he would not finish his term in office if he were to be elected President. He claimed Harrison would die and every Great Chief chosen every twenty years thereafter would also die. Hence, every President elected in a year ending in a zero would have his life terminated in some way.

In 1840 the cycle began as every President elected in a year ending in zero died in office! The only one escaping this so-called destiny was Ronald Reagan. However, an assassination attempt was made on his life.

Former Chief of Staff of the White House, Donald Regan, states in his book, *For the Record,* that during the Reagan Administration the use of astrology for major moves and decisions was influential. I personally find it fascinating that Ronald Reagan was the only president who may have taken some precautions metaphysically (beyond the realm of physical thought) and overcome a consecutive death cycle of 120 years! Could this be what saved this former President?

The Presidents elected in zero years since the onset of Tecumseh's Curse are as follows:

1. William Henry Harrison, elected 1840.
   Died of pneumonia in 1841.

2. Abraham Lincoln, elected 1860.
   Died by assassination in 1865.

3. James Abram Garfield, elected 1880.
   Died by assassination in 1881.

4. William McKinley, elected 1900.
   Died by assassination in 1901.

5. Warren Gamaliel Harding, elected 1920.
   Died from food poisoning in 1923.

6. Franklin Delano Roosevelt, elected 1940.
   Died from a stroke in 1945.

7. John Fitzgerald Kennedy, elected 1960.
   Died by assassination in 1963.

8. Ronald Wilson Reagan, elected 1980.
   Assassination attempt in 1981 (the only president to survive this curse).

9. George Walker Bush, elected 2000.
   Let us all have positive and protective thoughts for our current president.

This is an example of only one curse with very high statistics. The law of numbers dictates that the odds are just too towering for it to be coincidence.

Something other than a curse may have been the source of misfortune in the famous case of "King Tut's Curse." This alleged curse may have been the result of an allergic reaction to spores, a fungus-type particle, emanating from the tomb.

Many versions of this curse story exist but it basically goes as follows:

Tutankhamen was the ruler of Egypt from a very young age and died an early death at approximately nineteen. Howard Carter discovered his tomb in 1922. Supposedly, and with much controversy, it is said that a curse was written in hieroglyphics over the entrance that when translated read, "Death will slay with his wings whoever disturbs the peace of the Pharaoh." The tablet is claimed to have disappeared and no photograph or drawing was ever made of it. Many feel the tablet never existed, but the story was used as a means to keep away thieves.

Soon after the discovery, strange things started to happen and several of the scientists involved in the excavation were dying from mysterious causes shortly after entering the tomb. This is how the name "King Tut's Curse" was given birth. For years people believed this was indeed a curse as no other explanation was evident.

The media hype was enormous. Now, however, it has been discovered that there might be some scientific truth to the stories of the curse. According to German microbiologist Gotthard Kramer, the cause of these mysterious deaths may have been mold spores named *Aspergillus flavus* or *Cephalossporium*, a fungus-type bacteria. Mold spores can survive thousands of years even enclosed in a dry tomb. It is said most are harmless but some can be toxic. When the tombs were first opened, these spores may have been blown out into the air. If these spores enter the body through the nose, mouth, or eye mucous membranes, they can cause death through organ failure.

In fact, this is why archaeologists have started wearing masks and gloves for protection. The question remains: Did the Egyptians know about the effects of these mold spores? Even though the existence of mold spores has been proven, is this what really caused these mysteries deaths? Have the tabloids just made a great amount of money on stories about "The Mummy's Curse"?

Or did the Egyptians revere their Pharaohs so much like gods that their synergistic energies indeed established a curse to harm anyone who would disrupt their Pharaoh's final resting place?

Ponder these questions and make your own assessment, as these concepts are most thought provoking.

Many people feel curses exist only if you believe in them. Therefore, not to believe in curses is never to be cursed. To believe curses are nonexistent is a grand philosophy and I am all for it, as the mind is powerful and this belief in itself can keep you from harm's way.

But what about those who feel they have already fallen victim to a curse or have experienced such a plight before ever hearing this philosophy? Can they go back and change their thought? It is not always that easy. If we have been programmed in one belief, it is not easy to override it with new thought. If it were, habits would be broken in minutes.

For every 100 alleged curses that have been proved through science not to be a curse at all, there are another 100 curses that cannot be proved, having no logical explanation for the results. I personally do believe in the existence of curses. It is intense hatred launched with a tremendous amount of energy.

When speaking of general issues pertaining to the occult such as curses or the mysterious, Dion Fortune states it best in her book *Psychic Self-Defense,* remarking, "There cannot be so much smoke without some fire. It is not possible that the prestige of the magician in antiquity and the dread of the witch in the Middle Ages could have arisen without some basis in experience. The vapourings of the wise woman would be no more heeded than those of the village idiot if no painful consequences had ever been found to follow upon them."

Dion has a point. Has everyone through thousands of years made these matters up? Why would anyone give them any heed if there was not some truth connected to them?

I personally have seen firsthand the effects of such a hateful energy. I have come in contact with numerous people who have been enthralled by such trials.

The key is to know how to differentiate a real curse, hex, or evil spell from a period of confusion, or just having a "bad" day. Also, you must be aware of charlatans or phonies who will try to sell you on the fact that there is a curse on you when there is not, allowing them to financially gain from you.

Spells

Spells can be of a positive or a negative nature. Generally speaking, a magical spell is a formula that contains spoken, written, or chanted words; the burning of candles in various colors and layouts; incense burning; the casting of circles; the deployment of amulets, talismans, or charms; ritual baths; the sprinkling of salts, dusts, or flower petals; and symbolic statues or enactments.

Spells have many purposes and are very diversified. There are spells for everything: money, love, success, health, fertility, banishing, binding someone to stay away from you, or summoning up dead loved ones, spirits, and even demonic entities! Spells are typically used to fulfill something that someone wants in their life.

To cast a spell, you must have the proper intention and truly believe you can achieve it. I often hear people say they have continually tried to cast spells, have bought all the spell books, read all the articles, purchased all the spell kits, and end up disappointed. The reason I believe they are not successful is because their intention is not serious enough. Spells rarely should be used and only for very special purposes. Not merely to amuse you and friends on a Friday night.

Just like praying . . . I believe one single prayer to the God of your understanding with true intention is better than fifty prayers in which you just utter memorized words and don't think about the meaning behind the appeal.

Spells can be interesting and successful but should not be equated to having found an Aladdin's Lamp and, once executed, making wishes come true. They are an energy boost to the ears of the Universal Life Force. If you have tried to perform a "good" spell and have not encountered success, I suggest you rethink what you are expecting and how often you try.

If you try to cast spells weekly, you are depleting your own energy source and will not achieve much. You are asking so much that the Universe no longer pays attention to your call.

Negative spells should not even be considered. To try to cast a spell on someone for revenge or just to irritate him or her can indeed work, but be prepared. You may be very successful and feel you have acquired great skills of the occult. However, you will reap what you sow. Even if you are regretful after you purposely tried to harm someone or create an uncomfortable situation, you will still have to pay the penalty. It may not befall you immediately or in a few months but it will be building force to return to its sender! "Kill hate with kindness, not with hate!" This is true power!

What to Do if Threatened with a Hex, Curse, or Spell

Performing a hex, throwing a curse, or casting a harmful spell is not a simple task and few can successfully accomplish it. Therefore, if someone says they are going to put a curse on you, I would not take it too seriously and simply shrug it off as the words of an angry person. To panic is to open yourself up to assault. You may find it even laughable, and laughter can divert negativity. I mention laughter as a form of psychic defense later in this book.

A person applying a hex, curse, or harmful spell must have great knowledge and experience of the occult. The wannabe dark occultist or black magic practitioner will do him or herself more harm than good. Without control, direction, and knowledge, the curse will come back at them. It's like aiming a weapon at yourself when you think it is aimed at the victim. Reading a document on how to curse someone will not prepare you to lay a curse.

I have even seen it advertised that for a certain dollar amount one could have a curse put on someone via the Internet! Please! Again, I do believe in the existence of hexes, curses, and harmful spells but not for $19.99 plus free shipping and handling! Who would want to suffer the karma or the "what goes around comes around" theory of selling or laying curses? Therefore, I would not endeavor to describe how to perform such a doom. But I will tell you, to perform a hex, curse, or harmful spell you must unite with another energy not of this plane. One must go down into the "soot of the cauldron," so to speak, or "dance with the devil."

Although I believe that very few can actually execute a true and powerful evil affliction, do not let your guard down. If you think you have had an encounter with an individual or group that has such loathing for you, beware. They may have discovered

ways and means to penetrate your natural protective energy field
or aura.

Do You Have a Curse, Hex, or Evil Spell on You?

The likelihood is no, but for the very exceptional that may, here
is what to look for. Do not be overdramatic in summation by trying
to make your circumstances fit the symptoms. I find some people
love to be martyrs or want to use the excuse that they have a curse
on them to explain laziness, being unsuccessful, never finding the
right partner, always being in financial debt, and generally not creating their own positive environment in which to grasp a rewarding lifestyle. These things are not an indication of a curse but an
indication that you are not paying attention to the signals that the
universal power is sending you.

A hex, curse, or harmful spell usually is thrown for revenge. So
the first thing to think about is whether someone might have reason to seek revenge against you for a traumatic situation you may
have caused them in their life or in the life of someone close to
them.

This is not the fellow whose parking space you took or the single girl whose boyfriend you stole away at the Christmas party!
These are people who would wish you dead or to suffer a terrible
fate. Think about it. Most of us who were ever in a committed relationship have an ex-partner somewhere. Maybe we don't care for
that person or would like to see them "pay." But usually we do not
really wish them true death or injury! At least not after time.

Go back into your childhood or adolescence and try to remember if you did something that could still be lingering on in someone
else's mind. If you recall an act that you feel may have hurt someone on some level, you must apologize in some form for that action. Even if you do not ask forgiveness in person, you must truly
be regretful. By virtue of the fact that you are self-effacing, the person you mistreated should have no great power over you.
However, in some cases, he or she may still be the culprit.

How long do you feel you may have had "bad luck"—be it

deaths in families, illnesses, injuries, or repeated calamities? Sometimes this is not health related, but ill fates such as fires, natural weather disasters, thefts, and so forth may be due to a hex, curse, or spell. Things such as hair loss, job loss, routine illness, and other mundane occurrences can be a result of negative energy, not full-blown black magic.

Ask yourself a few questions and answer honestly.

1. Do you try to improve yourself or do you wait for others to help you?

2. Are you always complaining or keeping things to yourself?

3. Do you try to see the bright side to all negative situations or dwell only on the nonaffirmative?

If you suffer from the "poor me" syndrome, you may be causing your own misfortune and feeding the negativity around you. Therefore, what you think is a curse is just your own self-pity returning to you.

In your heart, you know if you have been the cause of your own misfortune or if you feel intuitively there is something that is not of this plane at work in a corrupt and sinister way. If this is the case, I provide for you the way to lift a curse, hex, or evil spell.

How to Lift a Hex, Curse, or Spell (Nondenominational)

It is not possible to render people powerless, but it is possible to render them unable to use their power against you.

A few notes before we begin. Remember you are performing this ritual under the assumption you are the victim of a genuine hex, curse, or harmful spell. If this does not prove to be successful, take another look at what you can do in your own life by means of ambition, activity, and alternative methods that can enhance your daily existence. This is a very powerful method that has proven to be successful, as my family was victim of a curse that I lifted.

Also, clients and the like have testimonies of its success. This does not follow any religious standard but may be said to be a spiritual combination of many belief systems. It was passed on to me from generations of intuitives, and I offer it to you in its original format. I do not believe in reinventing the wheel and have neither added nor deleted any part of this ritual.

The Timing

The moon must be dark, meaning the two or three days when the moon is not visible in the sky at all, regardless of weather. After a full moon, the moon starts to wane (decrease in size) and becomes smaller and smaller until there is no sight of it at all. This is a dark moon and the time you must perform the ritual. After those few days, the moon begins to wax, meaning you will see that first sliver of a crescent moon and it will begin to grow from there.

If you see any sign of the moon at all, it is too late. Keep in mind, this ritual *will not work* under a full, waning, or waxing moon. Even your intention will not be enough to release a hex, curse, or harmful spell. That leaves you only this two-to-three-day period a month in which to render these vibrations harmless. It may take planning and scheduling and be not at all convenient for *you*, but the universe and nature do not work around your agenda! If you miss it one month, you must wait and try again the next. There are no substitutes for nature. If this is important to you, you will find a way.

The Place

Be by yourself or have the ability to go to another room where no one will disturb you. If you live alone, you will not have a problem. If you have a family that does not understand what you are attempting to do and needs constant attention, you will have to be creative.

Go to a friend's house, escape to a bathroom, rent a motel room, or go to a safe remote area outside (always be safe and remember this can be done during the day). You must have zero interruptions.

If you are in a home office or spare room and a phone rings or a husband, wife, significant other, child, roommate, etc., interrupts you for any reason, the ritual is broken and you will have to start from scratch. No one must utter a single word to you. Sounds of nature or traffic are acceptable, as they are not directed specifically toward you. If you are interrupted, you can try again within minutes if you choose or later that day. Unplug phones, faxes, and pagers, and ask everyone around not to disturb you. Do all you can for total privacy.

Items You Will Need (No Choices)

Sorry if you feel I am being too tough but again there are no alternatives for the following and I do this in love to break this negativity forever! As an ex-victim of a curse myself, I understand what you are going through and the effort is well worth the outcome.

If these items are difficult to come by, take time and find them . . . no substitutes.

A Dull or Pointed "Nice Knife"

The idea is something that can cut. It can be as dramatic as a dagger, a sword, or an athame or as simple as a butter, steak, or dinner knife. I have used grapefruit knives and even letter openers. The idea is something that can cut through something else. A butter knife cuts through butter, a letter opener cuts through an envelope, a pâté knife cuts through pâté, and so forth.

Do not use a wand. By definition, it must be a knife, but one never used to hurt or harm someone. A "nice" knife!

Candles

Dinner candles only. No votive, no homemade, no scented, no decorative. One white. Not yellow, or off-white, but white (representing you). Rounded only, not square. At least six inches tall or over. Four more dinner candles: red, (representing the passion of the curse); pink (representing your love of yourself, others, and life); dark blue (representing the healing of your psyche and aura, and the damage that has already been done); and yellow (representing the attraction of the etheric—not of this world—to protect you from future attack).

Each candle needs a holder. It can be anything that will keep it straight, from a regular candlestick holder to a jelly glass or a piece of clay or earth. Design, color, or intricate detail makes no difference. The holders can be all different heights and shapes. However, the white candle must be in a holder that elevates it higher than the others. Put a brick, pedestal, or even a phone book under it, anything to bring up the height. It must be at least three inches taller than the other candles.

It does not make a difference what the heights of the other candles are. Only the white one, as this represents you. You are taking a stand and must dominate. I will explain the placement of the candles later.

Note: Also include matches or a lighter and a candle snuffer, cup, rock, shell, or something to extinguish your candles if you don't want to use your knife to put out candles.

Sea Salt

Table salt will not do! It must be sea salt. Most grocery stores or health food stores sell it. Coarse only, the kind you would put in a salt grinder.

Often we see the use of salts in rituals, ceremonies, or rites. However, other than it being from water and obviously natural, an explanation seldom accompanies the reason behind it. So I include for you the reason sea salt is used in this ritual.

Salt has always been a valued and respected commodity. Wars have been fought over salt, and spiritual references from our ancients address salt. Homer called salt "divine," and Plato referred to it as a "substance dear to the gods." Salt has been known to have sacred properties as it prevents decay, preserves, and protects. The Bible pronounces, "We are the salt of the earth." Throughout history salt has had many purposes. It preserves and enhances the taste of food, and some religious rituals required all sacrifices to be salted before offered to God.

Salt never loses it taste. It may turn rock hard, but once loosened and used, it always tastes the same. It has a steady influence.

The reason sea salt is used as opposed to table salt is that table salt may have additives. For this ritual, we need the most natural salt available, as it will be stronger and not weakened through processing. Sea salt is used with the intention of keeping preserved what is good and drawing out what is negative. Hence, it draws out the evil passion of the hex, curse, or spell from the red candle. It protects the white candle (representing you). It blesses the yellow candle, attracting the assertive power of the etheric energies. The blue candle is preserved for continued healing. Finally, the pink candle is guarded so love in your life does not decay.

Area to Set Up

Use a table or any flat surface. A coffee table, end table, card table, dresser or even two bricks with a sheet of plywood would suffice. Be imaginative; put a piece of wood across the bathroom sink, or use the top of a suitcase, a cutting board, or a cookie sheet if you must. Think and you will find a solution. It is important that the surface you utilize has the capacity to contain five candles. Employ the ground or floor if you don't mind bending. Experiment before your ritual, and if the chosen surface cannot hold all the items, find something different.

For those of you who feel this is a lot of work, realize what you are dealing with. Going to a grocery store to buy a few candles and a little sea salt is not much trouble compared to the curse thrown on you! So don't be lazy and do not feel you are inconvenienced. Just do it without complaint and tell no one, unless they are helping you.

Telling Others / Including Others

If you chose to tell others your intention, that is fine. But tell only those that are like-minded or at least respect your attempts and beliefs. If you would like to include another person or small group in your ritual, this is totally acceptable. Everything still remains the same. Do not have over four people conducting this ritual, as there would be too many energies involved. Also, even if you want others to help you, you can do only one curse removal at a moon phase. Meaning, if you think you have a curse and are with one or more people who also think they have a curse, only one per group can be addressed. You do not take turns releasing curses all in one sitting. There is no "now it's your turn" in one day. Focus on one curse, hex, or spell at a time.

Can Someone Remove a Curse for Another Person?

Yes, someone else can remove a curse for you. Even though we all have the ability to do this for ourselves, sometimes we are too close to the problem to resolve it. You may have the ability to remove it but you may also need a bit of help from a friend or like-minded person. Do not pay strangers to remove a curse unless you have reason to trust them and feel their intentions are true.

Hex-, Curse-, or Spell-Banishing Ritual

On the night of a dark moon, have all of your items at hand: table or platform, candles in holders, sea salt, knife, and matches or lighter. Do not light any incense, play music, or add anything of your own thoughts to this ritual. Stand for the entire process, unless physically you are unable. This is the only exception. Cast a circle by pointing your knife to the north and drawing an imaginary circle around yourself and your tools. Turn counterclockwise.

Place your white candle in the middle of your table or platform. Remember that it must stand three inches higher than the others. Place the other candles as follows:

The red to the left of the white candle.
The yellow above the white candle.
The blue to the right of the white candle.
The pink at the base or under the white candle.

Sprinkle your sea salt around each candle individually in a circle. It does not have to be perfect. Say nothing.
Light your candles in the same order you encompassed them

with salt: white, red, yellow, blue, pink. Step back approximately twelve inches from your table or platform. Hold your knife as firmly and carefully as you can with both hands and stretch it as far out in front of you as possible, chest high. Keeping your arms as straight as possible, still holding your knife, bring your arms slowly up until they are over your head. If you cannot get your arms totally over your head, come as close as you can. Do not push your limits.

With your arms and knife pointing directly toward the sky or ceiling, say out loud or whisper:

From this time on, all evil be gone, that has plagued this situation. Power on power, I cut all wickedness and cast it to the flame. It is no more. It is no more. It is no more. Crosses, eights, and ex's.

These words can be copied and set on the table in front of you or in a place you can see them. If you choose to memorize them, that is fine but not necessary. "Crosses, eights, and ex's" must be recited as above but the meaning is for you to decipher.

Now slowly bring your knife down and touch the flames of each candle (not extinguishing them) and in order: white, red, yellow, blue, pink. Finally, using your knife, candle snuffer, cup, rock, or shell, extinguish your candles in the same order. Do not blow out your candles as your breath is a creative energy and now is not the time to create. Visualize your circle ascending up until over your head and gone.

Helpful Hints

- When one or more people are executing this ritual, designate one person to do the physical part but the entire group should say the words, standing next to, partially around, or behind the primary facilitator. No one should ever stand in front of the main person, as this will block the flow of energy.

- It does not matter if lights are on in the room or not.

- The use of a tablecloth or some type of covering is optional and color is not important.

- The sea salt can be put into a bowl or poured from the container in which it was purchased.

- Do not fast on this day. Eat normally.

- Animals may be present providing they do not disrupt you.

- If interrupted, you must start over from the beginning.

- Immediately after the conclusion of this ceremony, clean your entire area and leave no trace of your setting. Do not use the candles or sea salt again; throw them all away.

Within twenty minutes you should feel the difference in energy around yourself or the person or people you have eased. Rest if possible. The next day perform one of the White Light Protection Techniques in Chapter 14, but wait at least twenty-four hours as you are still purging, and the dismissal of negative energy around you in itself is protection.

PART II

Dangers From the Departed

CHAPTER 5

Ghosts and How I Developed My Forms of Protection

Ghosts! What a feeling the mere word conjures up for us! Shadowy figures that saunter through cemeteries on moonless nights. A castle fallen into ruin encompassed with fog near a small town in England. A ghostly warrior riding through a Scottish countryside or other lands of legends.

Everyone loves a great ghost story, but once you have had a real paranormal experience, those stories can become reminders, and are then not so entertaining.

We have several names for these entities:

A *poltergeist* is a "noisy spirit." These are the restless souls that rattle and shake pots and pans and create noise to get attention. They are strong and take joy in annoying and upsetting people. Some consider them evil.

An *apparition* is an entity of a different nature, making no noise or sound. They appear and soon after vanish. They move through walls and can have a vaporous look. Usually they come for a purpose and mean no harm. It may be a recently dead loved one saying their last goodbye. It could be a long-departed soul who has come back to give you a message they hope you will understand telepathically or intuitively.

A *specter* is a haunting or disturbing image, one that comes back repeatedly. You hear the sounds of footsteps in the corridor when no one is present. The steps on a staircase buckle as if someone were on them, when no one is actually there.

This intruder inhabits a specific building or location. Perhaps because there is a strong connection there, it cannot let go and thus keeps returning. This recurring phantom reveals itself only over time. It normally has no connection from its lifetime to those inhabitants who encounter it.

For the most part, we generally categorize these lifeless souls under one heading: "Ghosts." Some people may never lay eyes on an apparition in their lifetime and others may see many of them. It just depends on where you live, where you go, and who on the other side may have something to communicate to you.

For centuries people have been afraid of ghosts, and all cultures have some type of ghost-fear burial rituals or ceremonies to protect the living from being haunted. Buddhist cultures of the Himalayas would write the name of the deceased on a piece of bamboo paper and then burn it. Other effects could be added as well.

This rite was meant to assure safe passage and the release of the soul in order for it to pursue its next incarnation. This would also ensure that the departed would not come back to haunt the living.

In the West Indies it is said that male ghosts return to be with their wives. For this reason, throughout the mourning period, the widows wear red underwear, as red is said to ward off ghosts!

Tribal dances, funeral customs, and incantations around the world are practiced in different manners. However, the ultimate purpose is the same: to isolate the living from the dead.

Many people in the Western world today who are skeptics, having no belief in ghosts, the paranormal, or things not of the psychical, will still wear black to funerals. They should know that the original belief in black being a color of mourning was taken from the idea that black made the living invisible to the dead!

When I was growing up, the idea of ghosts was not discussed much in our household. I was aware of the concept but never took it too seriously. Ghosts were the images you taped on your front window around Halloween. They were stories you told in the Girl Scouts around a campfire to make everyone scared.

However, this indifference drastically changed. One evening when I was approximately twelve years old, my mother, sister, and I were watching television. I decided to go to the kitchen to get a Coke. "Don't go in the kitchen!" my mother stated firmly.

I could not for the life of me figure out why I could not go into the kitchen. I was raised in this house and going into the kitchen was never an issue. The floor was not wet; we were not watching an educational show that could have ruined my life if I did not see the end. So what was it?

Strangely enough, I did not question my mother but just sat down. My mother sat very still. Ten minutes later she arose and carefully went toward the kitchen.

She peeked in as if to see if the coast was clear. But clear from what, I wondered? She then smiled and said, "Okay, if you want to come in, now you can." I went in, looked around, and saw nothing unusual. Perhaps she was hiding some type of present or gift from me. That must have been the case.

Weeks later, I decided to go up in the attic, where I used to keep some of my personal things and spend time with friends, as it had been made into a functioning space. I normally did not go in the attic at night, but only because our television was downstairs and I thought of it mostly as a daytime place.

This particular day I decided to bring a few things down after dark. My mother was working and my sister was on the telephone downstairs.

I walked up the attic stairs and in the dark felt around for the light fixture hanging from the ceiling. It was a bit of a walk to get to that fixture and I walked in total darkness for several seconds.

Our attic was divided into two sections. The first part was where the light was located, a gray and dreary area, which we used for storage. The second half of the attic had double doors, which led to a dark but pleasant room with a window.

As I turned on the light, I instantly felt a chill or change in temperature, but saw nothing. As I glanced at the double doors where I intended to go, I thought I had seen a blur of a tall skinny man wearing a hat.

I turned around and ran down the stairs, not stopping to shut off the light. I told my sister nothing, and when my mother came home from work, I said nothing.

My mother could see from the street below that the attic light was on and inquired about it. I explained I had forgotten to shut it off. "You shouldn't go up there at night," she stated.

"Why?" I asked.

"The lighting is not good and you could fall," my mother replied. "Don't worry about the light. We'll turn it off tomorrow."

To prove there was nothing wrong, as we were three women living alone, I insisted I would just go upstairs and simply shut it off. My mother waited for me at the bottom of the staircase as if I were going to war. I didn't even look, shut the light off, and ran downstairs.

As days passed, I would see this apparition often, sometimes downstairs on the porch that led to our attic and sometimes in the kitchen. It was always the same. A tall skinny man, a drawn face with a hat and casual clothes. I figured out shortly that my mother must have seen him too, but did not want to frighten us. My older sister appeared oblivious to all of this. I learned later, however, that both my sister and my mother had also seen apparitions.

Being raised Catholic, I prayed that the tall, skinny man would go away and leave us alone. My prayers gave me comfort at night and my sleep was never interrupted. I was convinced that the holy water fountain I kept at the entrance of my room kept me safe. Things were fine . . . for a while.

Then, one sunny afternoon my mother, sister, and I were sitting at the kitchen table. From the kitchen you could see the entrance to the attic. Suddenly, out of nowhere, we all saw the apparition. Within seconds it was gone. No one said anything.

At this time I decided something must be done, but what? I had no knowledge of ghosts and frankly didn't want any. It was at this point I knew that there had to be a way to get rid of it so I thought I would make something up.

All procedures, cures, and remedies had to be developed by someone, so why not by me? I decided that I would find a way to rid the house of this specter!

I prayed, but that did not seem to be enough. That was only a "quick fix" and not long-lasting. Using common sense, I decided that maybe he was unable to move on.

The next day I left the window of the attic open so he might escape and go to what I now call the other side. Although it was a good attempt, I did not meet with success.

Trying to resolve this dilemma, I would sit for hours on our couch in a state of meditation. However, at the time I didn't realize that I was actually practicing meditation. Finally it came to me!

I saw a white light in my altered state of consciousness. I determined it was that light the apparition needed to go to, as this was the porthole to the other side. I felt the light signified refuge.

I saw it as a means of transition to a protected, peaceful eternity.

Soon after discovering that the house had more than one lost soul, I developed a way of taking these entities to the other side, "to the light."

At some point during daylight hours only, as nighttime seemed too ominous, I would lie on my back on the bed. Without crossing my legs or arms, I would place the palms of my hands downward. Then with my eyes closed, I would envision a blanket of white light slowly covering me from a few inches below my toes to a few inches above my head.

This shield was my form of protection and strength, so I would be more powerful against any opposing forces, before I would start my procedure.

Next, I would visualize where I thought an entity might be in the house. If I could not get a sense of a presence, I would stop and try again another day. I felt apparitions would come and go through some type of vortex in the house. If they were not present, I could not remove them. If I did feel a nearness, I would proceed.

Subsequently, I would then visualize myself out of my physical body, sending my etheric body to stand directly next to who or whatever it was I was going to send to the light. I would see myself with one white glove on my left hand as yet another form of protection, as I did not want to touch the essence of this nonliving being.

Then I would take the entity by its right hand and ascend upward slowly on an approximately 45-degree angle. I would see us pass through the roof of the house, through the clouds (regardless of weather), through the atmosphere, through outer space until I saw a white light that looked like a tunnel or shaft.

I would release his hand at the very edge of the tunnel and tell him to continue on and follow the light. I would *never* go into the tunnel, as it is not anyone's place to do so. If you try to enter the light before you are called to it, I believe you will be propelled out.

After I sent a lost soul on his way, I would descend back into my body and remove myself from the altered state of consciousness. I would then see the blanket of white light roll back and disappear. At this point I would bestow a new white light around me. I would stand up straight and see it descending upon me from my head to my toes.

When I finally felt the house was entirely cleared, I surrounded it daily with a sphere of white light so it would repel these entities and not allow them to return. There has been total peace in that home ever since.

I obviously believe some earthbound entities need help to get to the other side, where they belong. These are the lost entities who cannot find the light and *want* to make the transition. Some beings find the transition more difficult than others: it is as though they became disoriented on their way to a higher plane. Occasionally, when I would encounter an apparition that was troublesome, I would call upon an angel to help me guide the spirit to peace.

Bear in mind, the souls I speak about are merely bewildered and need direction. However, when dealing with extreme situations of the paranormal, it is always wise to consult with professionals.

CHAPTER 6

Buildings That Retain Negative Energy

There was a dreary mist encircling the Blue Ridge Mountains. The summer skies in North Carolina were filled with clouds. The storm shrieked with thunder as if it were suffering.

A newly built log cabin stood solitary and powerful against the mountains. This home belonged to Janet and Raymond Spear, business associates and friends of mine who had just moved from Florida. They had been waiting for a year and a half for the building process to be completed. The Spears stood in front of their home with umbrellas in their hands and smiles on their faces.

They opened the rustic door and entered with great anticipation. Everything was exactly as planned yet they had an overwhelming feeling of doom. Attributing this emotion to the weather, they looked around and saw the builders had done an excellent job.

"When the sun shines tomorrow, we will feel much better." Raymond said. The sun did come out the next day and yet they still both shared a mutual sense of sorrow.

Janet went into the kitchen to make breakfast and the pendulum clock she had placed on the wall the day before came crashing to the floor. She dismissed it by explaining she did not use the proper kind of nail and probably did not hit the stud in the wall.

While in the process of mixing ingredients to make an omelette, a box of dishes suddenly fell off the counter, breaking everything inside. "I hope this house isn't haunted," she laughed. "How could

it be?" said Raymond. "It's brand new and the land never had anything on it. No burial grounds, no wars, and no deaths. I researched the area before we ever bought the lot. We're just going
through the adjustments that one experiences in a new house."

A series of strange occurrences took place over the next several
weeks. Although they knew they should have been happy and excited, they somehow never felt comfortable.

When the home was finally settled and all the furnishings from
pictures to plants were in place, they still were left feeling disappointed. The Spears never felt a presence of anything supernatural.
It was just a presence of an angry type of intensity. They felt un-
welcome yet didn't know why.

I eventually went to visit them and, having no sense of direction, got lost. As the Universe works in strange ways, I ventured
upon a man hiking and asked directions to the new house that had
just been built. He pointed up the road and frowned. "Do you live
around here?" I questioned.

"Yep, I sure do," he uttered.

"Beautiful area, isn't it?" I added.

"Used to be," he said.

"Why is that? Has something happened to change it?"

"No, the area hasn't changed but my view has," he concluded.

He continued on to say that the house I was looking for now
blocked his view. He watched it being built for over a year, and
every day more of his beautiful scenery was taken away. Finally it
was all gone! After further conversation, I learned he had watched
for hours through binoculars as the builders assembled my friends'
home.

At this point I was still not aware the Spears had any kind of
anxiety about their new log cabin. How could a log cabin take
away much of a view anyway? I thought. As I drove up the drive-
way, I realized it was on stilts and I could understand the man's an-
noyance. I entered their home and there stood Raymond and Janet
at the front door. They smiled and give me welcoming hugs. The
house was beautiful. It was bright and cheery, yet something felt
wrong. I tried not to pay much attention to what I was feeling as I
was tired from driving and wanted to rest.

I said nothing and just visited. Finally, Janet couldn't wait any
longer. "Do you feel anything strange in this house?" she asked.

"Well, what exactly do you mean?" I replied.

"We were hoping you would feel what we're feeling and may have an answer." I admitted there was anger about the place and that it wasn't the cozy abode I had anticipated.

I informed them about the man who had had his view taken away. His obsessive energy must have become so strongly negative that he projected hostility through vibration, right into the house. His anger had penetrated the walls and floors and ceilings. The nails and grout had absorbed his loathing.

Raymond asked me what they could do about this situation. There were many rituals, blessings, and clearing of space that I could have performed but that was not the entire answer, not for this particular space. The reason none of these solutions would work was because the negativity would have come back over and over as the man would keep projecting his thoughts at them. They needed something that would correct the situation and then fill the void with love.

The next day I decided to hike over to this gentleman's home. He was outside and quite elderly yet physically fit.

"Remember me?" I asked.

"Oh yes," he said with a bit of a smile.

"My friends had no idea they were blocking anyone's view. Your house is so hidden they didn't even know they had a neighbor." He did not reply.

I determined he lived alone and had few friends. Later that day, after remembering his last name, I called Information and got his phone number. We called and invited him over for dinner. He refused at first, but I was somehow able to persuade him to join us. As a result, all became friends and the Spears offered to assist him in any way they could if he ever had a problem. Janet and Raymond also decided they would have him over to visit with them when possible. I could see their neighbor's dislike was gone. He also recognized the advantages of having younger people around him who might give him help if needed.

Knowing he would no longer continue to project arrows of revenge, I performed a smudging ceremony, as I still needed to remove the energy that was present.

For this I simply used a smudge stick of white sage. I cleared the house of the energy he projected and it has never come back. I explain in detail this smudging ritual in Chapter 10: "Rituals and Ceremonies."

Often people feel a house or building is haunted when it is just carrying energy from previous owners or projected thoughts, as in the case of the Spears.

Another common example is when we enter the home of a couple who show no outward signs of arguing and appear to be happy. However, you can "just feel" that they must have been fighting before you rang the doorbell.

The expression "The tension was so thick in the room, you could cut it with a knife" is not new to any of us. Consciously or subconsciously we have all felt the aftermath of buildings retaining emotional upheaval.

People will often assume that only old houses hold peculiar or strange vibrations. We also may conclude that a place where someone had died or was hurt intentionally gives off these emanations of secrecy and darkness. But this is not solely the case.

A couple who owned a bed-and-breakfast establishment in New Orleans would one day have sensations of depression and the next day they would be fine. They had no psychological disorders or other problems, but this feeling would continue to beset them both at the same time.

What these proprietors were experiencing was a "hiccup in time," a negative energy from the past that had reentered their dwelling. However, none of the deceased people who were involved would return as ghosts—just this recurring vibration.

These kinds of negative vibrations tend to stay dormant for a while and then slowly start to rise back into the establishment. Once they run full course, they then retreat, but return later on to continually create a disturbing cycle.

Areas such as this need to be cleared. Yet, they can be cleared only when the frequency is high and the negative vibration is present. Compare it to a leaky roof. It may be hard to tell where a roof is leaking until you wait for it to rain. Then, you know what you're dealing with and it can be fixed. Intuitives and sensitives can pick up these fluctuations easily. But even if you are not advanced in such matters, you can still train yourself to be more aware of the emotional atmosphere around you.

My grandfather taught me to sense an environment by being

mindful of my own breathing. It is so simple but very few of us notice it.

When you enter a building for the first time, immediately pay attention to see if your breathing has changed. Is it faster, slower, restricted, or easier?

If it is faster, there is most likely something that your body senses to be fearful of or even dangerous. However, the more positive side of rapid breathing is that it could indicate something fascinating and exciting goes on in this location. Slow breathing, on the other hand, can indicate peace, tranquillity, and high levels of spirituality such as is found in a church, a house of worship, or perhaps the home of people who are on a very spiritual path.

If you feel restricted and suddenly have a difficult time breathing, this could mean people in this site feel trapped or stuck. You will find this in business offices or retail stores where the employees are not happy and anxious for the day to end.

Easy breathing is plain to figure out. At these locations all is usually well and there is a balance of the mental, the physical, and the spiritual.

Evaluating your own home can be a bit tricky. When you have lived in a place for a time, it is hard to get an impression as you have grown accustomed to it. So before you move into a new home, you must pay attention from the beginning to your breathing. This method of discerning vibrations is best for first impressions or a place you have not visited too often.

Your body's reaction is also a means of providing you with an honest emotional meter. We all know our bodies don't lie. They have built-in warning systems that are meant to keep us safe. We must remember to tune into them and listen. Consequently, in addition to noticing your breathing changes when entering a home or building, note how you begin to feel physically. Try not to have any preconceived notions. Enter with a clear state of mind. Then, see what you start to experience. Cheerfulness, sadness, reflection, or anxiety.

This combined with reading your breathing will give you quite an accurate picture of the energy that a place retains. It will speed up your decision-making process as to whether you want to stay in a building for any period of time or leave shortly.

Practice this whenever you get the chance. It can make a trip to what you thought may be a boring place a bit more interesting. Now you have something to decipher once you enter.

After a while you will also be able to tune in to vibrations in the offing that have not reached a location yet. Have you ever said to anyone, "I don't want to stay here too long. I have a feeling something awful is going to happen"?

We can even sense parking spaces. "I just didn't have a good feeling about parking there so I parked further down."

By paying attention to our bodies and using our psychic agility, we can pick up forces that may well keep us from harm's way and judge the environment of a place more accurately.

CHAPTER 7

Possession and Walk-Ins

Possession and walk-ins are two entirely different entities. Becoming possessed by something means the possession takes place without permission and is an invasion for baneful purposes. These evil forces may be intruders from the beyond that never had physical form and now need a body to conduct a specific action. Some religions believe that demonic forces attempt to possess innocent people in order to torment or destroy them.

A walk-in, on the other hand, is a soul with whom we have made an agreement. It wants to "walk into" our body as we walk out. This is another option for entering the earth. No physical death occurs but personality changes do. It is not necessary to protect ourselves from walk-ins, as they do not have the ability or inclination to enter unless our souls agree. This is a free-will choice.

Possession

In cases of possession, exorcism, which is a rite that drives away evil spirits or the Devil, is performed by a religious figure. Authorized by the Roman Catholic Church, an actual exorcism rite was written in approximately 1614 under Pope Paul V. In this ritual it was emphasized that a priest should not perform exorcisms on people who were not truly possessed. As the medical field advanced, logical causes for what appeared as demonic possession were discovered. It was difficult to distinguish a truly possessed individual from someone with schizophrenia, multiple personalities, or other psychological disorders.

There are several variations of exorcisms. Typically, when a priest or spiritual figure performs an exorcism, he is rarely alone. Usually three or more people are there to assist him in this banishment. A second person is included as a backup if the exorcist should die. A third person, typically from the medical profession, assists the exorcist. Also, sometimes a family member of the victim is included as an overseer to witness the procedure.

It is said that water dissipates the power of an evil spirit, and as we are "the salt of the earth," usually water and salt are included in exorcism. Prescribed prayers are also recited and the demon is told to depart from the victim. If the demon does not leave the victim, the ritual is performed again until the evil spirit is cast out.

Regardless of religious persuasion, my personal interviews and research in this area have led to the following conclusion: The recommended items of guardianship from demonic possession include displayed crucifixes, Bibles, holy water, and any religious statue depicting a saint or any religious object encouraging the belief in Jesus Christ. Some people feel that merely saying the words "Jesus, Jesus, Jesus" is also a form of dispelling possible detriment.

If a possession were to take place, it would most likely happen when a person was in a weakened state of being, perhaps from being depressed or suffering from substance abuse. This is because at such times their aura was weak and their defenses down. This fragile condition would allow an open door for such corruption of the body, mind, and spirit.

Very rarely are exorcisms performed anymore. In these modern times, most people seek assistance from psychological and medical professionals before consulting an exorcist. Nevertheless, in a universe so vast and so mysterious, I would not discount anything. I invariably consider all avenues, but I do always start with logic first.

Walk-Ins

Unlike the uninvited possession into a blameless body, I do believe that our bodies can be used as housing for gentle souls with whom we voluntarily want to switch places. Such is the case of a walk-in. I see it as an excellent way to incarnate. It is one of the three experiences we may have when we die.

The first of these experiences takes place if we have worked through all previous karma. If we have indeed learned our lessons and found the road back to our creator, we then have a choice. At this time we would have evolved through experiences on earth to the point that our souls are now prepared for the afterlife.

We no longer must make the journey back to this planet and rejoin our fellow man. Our souls are at the highest level of growth and now is the time to reap the benefits of the other side.

After death you are no longer obligated to return or reincarnate. You do not have to return to this planet ever again.

The second experience occurs if karma has not been fulfilled. When we still have many lessons to master and have repeated many mistakes from lifetime to lifetime, we must return to try again.

We are still attempting to correct old karma. This does not necessarily mean we must suffer and live dreadful lives. We need to keep striving for development of our spirits.

In this case when we depart and our bodies die, we must reincarnate into a new body and begin our journey from birth all over. It's like taking a course in school: If you fail over and over again, the teacher does not pass you. You must accomplish the tasks required and reach the common goal of the class, just as the other pupils before you.

Some students pass the first time and others keep coming back time and time again. Each time we return to try once more, we are usually not situated in a similar lifestyle to the previous incarnation. We may still have a few similar interests, tastes, and dislikes. We may meet some of the same people we use to know, as they incarnated too. But basically, we may be of another race, religion, or sex and living in a totally different environment.

All circumstances on earth will be different each time. The more you learn in one lifetime, the fewer lifetimes you will have to return!

The third experience that may occur after death is if you decide to be a walk-in—a peculiar name for an interesting phenomenon. These are souls that have learned and evolved and volunteer to come back. They have a specific mission in mind or there is one more thing they feel they must accomplish.

All walk-ins in my conception are good. Walk-ins do not come back for evil purposes. As I mentioned earlier, evil beings possess people; they do not walk in.

When a soul has completed its purpose in this lifetime or it cannot continue to complete its mission, it may decide to leave before the physical body is ready to die. I am not referring to suicide. I mean making an agreement with another soul that wants to be here for a special purpose.

No one would see a physical difference at the beginning of this takeover, but family and friends may notice personality changes that are always for the better.

If a soul decides to walk out and allows another soul to walk in, the transfer must take place. There are many ways in which this can be done. Often someone will suffer an illness or injury. When a transfer like this occurs, it is easier for the entering soul to take position in the body as habitual functions are interrupted and the body's system is not routine. Therefore, it makes it smoother for the new soul to merge into the body.

Not only in physical illness can this transfer of spirit take place but also in psychological illness. An individual may go through a trauma or become very depressed, then suddenly without the use of chemicals he or she has a rebirth and looks forward to life with gusto and joy. He or she becomes a "new person" for no apparent reason.

On a more positive note, not all walk-ins enter through the tunnel of accidents, illness, and depression. This shift can occur through a meditative state or even while sleeping. To the outside world it appears as though these people have some type of revelation.

Walk-ins have great respect for the human body and for others. Although it takes them some time to adjust, once they do, they become very special people. In one year you may see someone quit smoking or drinking, lose weight, or become a Nobel Prize winner!

Recently I read a true story that depicted a race car driver who was in such a catastrophic accident he was almost totally paralyzed. No one thought he would be able to move again. After a certain period of time he had a miraculous comeback and is now running in triathlons! Walk-in? Who can be sure?

You have most likely experienced individuals who have made dramatic and positive changes in their lives, without the aid of counseling or any traumatic experience that would coax them into doing such a thing. They are "just not the same person." This is not to take any credit away from people who work hard to turn their lives around or those who benefit from counseling or treatment centers. I believe there are far more people who become motivated to change their lives by the strength of their own willpower, than there are walk-ins.

Some people have a spiritual experience, which may awaken something in them. Some may have a brush with death that gives them the zest for life again. Some may get tired of being unsuccessful and employ sheer determination. But then again, some may be walk-ins.

I have heard many people say, "I am not the same person I use to be. I changed three hundred and sixty degrees and I don't even remember how I did it."

The new soul that replaces the soul that has chosen to leave has no recollection of the transition. It may take the soul years to adjust to the new body and figure out what it is doing.

I have encountered many people who later in life express their feelings by saying things such as, "I still don't know what I'm here for. What's my purpose? I know I am supposed to be doing something, but what?"

Typically these are people who are wonderful and kind, spiritual and adventurous, but obviously perplexed. What they do not understand is that they may have incarnated into a body that has been on the planet for many years. Consequently, they did not have to experience birth, childhood, and adolescence.

However, they are in essence newly here and adjusting to their bodies. This adaptation can take a few years even though they have a special goal to accomplish. People will comment on occasion that years ago they made a choice to change their lives around and still have not gotten "their act together"!

They may have incarnated only a few years before and the period of adjustment is frustrating them. Once they adjust to their new form, the true purpose of their entry will unfold. To adjust they must consciously realize that their soul chose this body and is prepared to work with it as a partner to cocreate. When this happens, these individuals have the ability to make wondrous things come to pass.

CHAPTER 8

Toxic Past-Life Associations

Past-life associations can fool us! The belief that we have lived another lifetime and have returned again (as addressed in the previous section) can filter down to relationships that do not always make sense.

Many of my clients tell me they are in relationships with people they know are not right for them, but they just can't help it. Therefore, they believe it must be a "past-life thing." They feel there is unsolved business from another time and another place that must be completed. Sometimes this philosophy can be absolutely correct. Someone was taken away suddenly or tragically and we need to deal with the karma of this situation.

Often we come back in their lives to correct a wrong from another lifetime. However, that is not authorization to stay in a codependent relationship that is not good for either party.

I feel that many people use the concept of past-life relationships or associations as an excuse for not properly taking charge of their own lives. It is much easier to dismiss an action or circumstance using the belief that it must be a past-life problem. This is often easier to accept and explain than using logic and sound reasoning.

One of my clients, Michael, is married to a woman who is desperately needy. She is physically capable and thirty-two years of age, but she will not work, is overly emotional, and has the attitude that "the world owes her a living." Her husband is not a wealthy man and needs her help to generate more income and be supportive of him. However, he says nothing and is constantly manipulated by her demands and whims.

A psychologist would most likely refer to him as a "victim by choice." However, he tells me he owes his wife from a past life and is making up for it now! This attitude makes it easier for him to reject counseling and realistically deal with the situation. I suggested he perform a past-life regression. To do this he would have to go back in time in a somewhat hypnotic state to see if, in fact, he was acquainted or related to her in another lifetime.

He refused as he did not want another person around to hear what he had to say. He also was very uncomfortable having someone else placing him in a hypnotic state. He felt he could not trust anyone with such fragile issues.

Michael tried many methods of regressing himself through breathing, counting, and visualization, but to no avail. He finally concluded that the only way he could perform this action was to be talked through it. However, he still didn't want someone else involved.

I offered him a solution that I have been using for years with great success. Many of my clients have also found this approach to be an excellent method for regressing oneself in the most comfortable and nonintrusive way possible.

To perform a past-life regression by yourself, you will need two tape recorders and two audiotapes. Typically, we all trust the sound of our own voice. Therefore, you will record your own voice. This will furnish you with instructions that will put you into an altered state of consciousness.

This particular technique will assist you in determining whether you knew someone from a past life or not. It will also let you discover the circumstances that were involved.

Special note: If you do not want to reexperience any negative lifetime, you will not. However, before you begin the regression, say, "If the lifetime I am going to experience is one that is violent or upsetting, I do not want it known to me."

Sit down, and slowly and gently read into the tape recorder the following script I have written. Remember to allow enough silent time in between questions that will allow you to answer later.

Close your eyes . . .
Visualize a pale blue light ascending up your body . . .
See it entering through your toes . . . to your ankles . . .
Flowing up to your knees . . . to your thighs . . . to your hips . . .
Up to your chest . . . your shoulders and arms . . .
Your neck . . . your entire face . . . the top of your head . . .
Now breathe in slowly and exhale out loud . . .
Breathe in slowly and exhale out loud . . .
Breathe in slowly exhale out loud . . .

Now see yourself standing in front of a flowered archway . . .
The sky is sunny and there is green grass all around . . .
There are no buildings or people anywhere . . .
It looks like a radiant garden . . .

Slowly walk through the archway following a stone pathway
ahead of you . . .
You feel safe and peaceful . . .
Continue walking . . . slowly . . .
You see a waterfall in the distance . . .
It flows over a crystal mountain and is dazzling . . .
The path ends and right at your feet you see a stream . . . It is filled
with gemstones of amethyst, carnelian, and rose quartz . . .
These gemstones act as a base for the slow-moving water that
passes over them . . .
Stretched across the stream are three arched bridges in a row . . .
They are made of wood, strong and solid, having smooth lines . . .
One bridge is directly in front of you . . .
The next is three feet to your left . . .
The other three feet to your right . . .
Take a minute and examine the three bridges . . .

Pick the one you are drawn to at this time and focus your eyes on
the bridge . . .
Stand in front of the bridge you chose, but do not cross yet . . .
Do not cross until I tell you . . .

Okay . . . start to move slowly across the bridge you have
chosen . . .

As you cross, look at the water and gemstones below and how magical they appear . . .

Continue slowly across the bridge, occasionally glancing up at the waterfall ahead . . .
You are now coming to the end of the bridge . . .
You are now leaving the bridge . . .

Stop now and see the waterfall; it is nearly in front of you . . .
Take a few steps farther until you are facing the waterfall . . .
It flows into a tranquil pond surrounded by abundant fruit trees, willow trees, and nature.

Look around . . . you will see a golden bench with railroad tracks of crystal in front of it . . .
Sit on the bench . . .

In the distance you will see a white train with only an engine and one car . . .
The train stops in front of you . . .
Get on board . . .
The seats inside the train are made of red velvet, and golden tassels tie the matching red drapes back from the window . . .
Take a seat . . .
See the door closing . . .

The train is now moving quickly and travels back in time . . .
You cannot see out the windows but you can feel the motion . . .

The train comes to a halt and the door opens . . .
Remain seated . . .
A mist of fog is seen from the door and you cannot tell what is beyond . . .

Step carefully to the door, but do not get off . . .
The fog is still thick and you cannot see much . . .
Before stepping off the train, in silence, I want you to call [fill in name]'s name . . .
Have you called her or his name? . . .

Do you hear anyone male or female answer back? . . .

If you have, I want you to stay there in the doorway for a moment and just look into the fog . . .

If you have not, I want you to quickly close the door of the train, travel back to the garden, cross the bridge, then go through the archway and back into this room and wake up.

If you *have* heard a voice respond . . .
I want you to now step off the train . . .
The fog is starting to disappear and you will shortly see a scene . . .
Do not be afraid of what you see, as it could be anything . . .
Know you are perfectly safe and secure . . .

The fog is starting to lift more . . . and more . . .
You still cannot see much . . .
However, tell me, do you hear anything? . . .

The fog is now completely gone . . .
Tell me, what do you see? . . .
Walk into the scene . . .
Are you a male or a female? . . .
What do you look like? . . .
Tell me, what are you wearing? . . .
Tell me what you are looking at right now . . .

Okay . . . now you see three people in front of you; they are walking toward you . . .
What do these people look like? . . .
Do you know who they are? . . .

Tell me who you think they are, in that lifetime . . .
Choose one of these three people to talk to . . .
The one you have chosen male or female is the one known as [insert name of person in question] in your current lifetime in the twenty-first century . . .

There is bench in front of you . . .
You and this person must sit down . . .

Ask the person what his or her name is in that lifetime . . .
What did he or she say? . . .
Ask the person what he or she does in that lifetime . . .
What did the person say? . . .
Ask the person to allow you to see the story about the two of you in
that lifetime . . . and when you feel comfortable, tell me what you are
seeing . . .

If the information has not been seen or given, ask him (or her) how
you died . . .
What did he say? . . .
Ask him how he died . . .
What did he say? . . .

Ask him if he has any important messages or information for you.
Is he upset with you, happy with you, or does he feel you need to re-
solve something? . . .
What is he saying? . . .

Has this person come back into your new lifetime just to be near
you as a friend, relative, lover, or coworker, or is he someone merely
passing through? Is there something more? . . .
Tell me what the person says . . .
Thank him, then see yourself standing up . . .

Now see the train in front of you and get back on board . . .
Wave goodbye to the person you have spent time with and thank
him or her for the information and company . . .

Find a seat and sit down . . .
Feel the train moving . . .
The train stops and you are back at the waterfall . . .

Exit the train . . .
You now look the same as when you left . . .
Walk across the bridge . . .
Through the archway . . .

You are back where you started . . . in your chair . . .
Keep your eyes closed and feel you are refreshed . . .

At the count of three, open your eyes . . .
One . . . two . . . three . . . welcome back . . .

Once you have recorded this part of the process, you can immediately start your regression or save the tape for a later date.

When you decide to perform this process, go into an area where you will not be disturbed. You will need one cassette player to play the tape you already recorded and one to record the entire session. In essence you will have two machines in use at the same time. Sit in a chair, lie on a bed, or situate yourself in any sitting or lying position that is comfortable. Do not stand, as it is too tense. Allow yourself half an hour.

When you are set up, turn on the player you will be recording the session with and then turn on the player with the prerecorded regression.

After this regression you should know if you have indeed known the person you were querying about or not. This should also provide insights as to why you treat someone one way or the other.

As well as the way they treat you.

This is a means to correct or resolve old issues in order to guard yourself from continuing relationships that are futile. Or on the other hand, it may allow a new relationship to flourish.

Below are a few options that may be of interest. Of course, you can also vary this method as well.

Additional items to include can be candles, incense, or quiet instrumental background music. Candle colors, music, and types of incense are entirely up to you. Use what relaxes you. This should be a pleasurable experience.

Other things to consider are these:

If you don't mind someone else taking you through this process, ask a friend to help. Have them read directly from the book and record the session.

If you want to do this privately but do not care for the sound of your own voice or are not comfortable reading into a recorder, ask someone else to record it. Your friend can record the regression and give you the tape for a later date when you can work in privacy. This is a wonderful alternative, especially if you know someone who has a soothing voice. They never need to know the final result unless you choose to share it with them.

Other things to consider are the places or objects I recommend. If you should have a fear of trains, visualize a substitute: a bus, airplane, car, or boat. If you are not comfortable with any mode of transportation, see yourself walking down a road until you come to a small lookout area.

Use an alternative that puts you at ease. If you don't like waterfalls, see a mountain or a beautiful palace. There are no steadfast rules here.

That being said, and returning to the story of my client Michael, of whom I spoke earlier, he tried the regression and was very pleased.

As a result of his past-life regression, he and his wife went to counseling and a huge amount of pressure was lifted off him. His wife is now working and is not as domineering. When I asked him what happened in the regression that warranted such changes, he simply replied, "I never got off the train!"

Because we may have known someone in another lifetime, that does not allow them to take advantage of a situation. Sometimes we have a special fondness or love in our hearts and want to help someone else. This is totally different from feeling obligated, for this is love that has shone through from one life to the next.

I will often meet someone only once and feel an attachment to him or her. Although it may be a past-life association, that does not mean the person is to be part of my life this time.

A registered nurse once told me she worked at a hospital and daily would buy her dinner in the cafeteria. The cashier always had a smile and the nurse felt a special fondness for her. They never exchanged names or had any desire to socialize or even have much of a conversation. However, the RN felt that they may have been sisters in a past life and their energy just traveled in the same direction. For that reason, they were drawn to working in the same place.

Just as we can be drawn to strangers and acquaintances on a positive level, people who never did anything to us unjustly can also repel us. These are usually individuals we did not get along with in a past life who did someone wrong that upset both parties.

Be aware of past-life associations. Before you cast judgment, go to the root of the problem and find out the history that may have generated certain feelings and emotions. You may save yourself time and energy and protect yourself from making unfortunate mistakes.

PART III

Traditional Forms of Protection

CHAPTER 9

Prayers and Affirmations

When we pray, we ask; when we meditate, we listen. All faiths believe in prayer of some kind. We pray to ask for protection, to give thanks, and to prevent negativity.

The power of prayer is one of the most effective ways of psychic defense. It does not matter of what faith you are or if you are of any faith at all. Your prayers can be those that were established decades ago and that were handed down and memorized since childhood.

They can be words we have written ourselves that promote a positive mental attitude. There are many words for God. Whether you pray to the God of your understanding or pray to yourself, it is an issue of faith and faith is trust. To this day, I say evening prayers and I always ask that I and the people I love be free from injury, danger, or any negative forces.

I pray and surround myself with a hue of white light that covers my entire body. I not only feel safe, but also feel at liberty to request what it is I desire, when necessary. It may be health, work, protection for others, or even a well-earned vacation!

I do not believe we were put on this planet to suffer. Life should be interesting and fun. We can still grow spiritually and enjoy ourselves at the same time. This is balance . . . this is cosmic law.

What a gloomy energy would encompass the earth if we all were serious and no one laughed, celebrated, or enjoyed some earthly pleasures!

As long as you equalize fun, property, success, and financial security with love, prayer, thanks, and helping your fellow man, you are balanced. Therefóre, when you pray, do not be afraid to ask for yourself. You are not being selfish or material. You are creating an equilibrium of energy . . . the yin and the yang; the feminine and the masculine; the positive and the negative; the light and the dark.

While attending a lecture on spirituality in North Carolina, a plain-looking woman raised her hand and asked why the lecturer had advised the audience, "Ask and you shall receive." She complained, "Why is everyone so concerned with the material here? I thought I was in a group of metaphysical individuals who were beyond such pettiness. Should not the love of God or the Godhead be more important than such earthly things?"

From what I could see, she was actually looking for an argument. The speaker said he was going to approach this issue later in his speech and to please be patient as he would explain later. She did not like that response and left the room.

I discreetly followed her out into the corridor. "Are you leaving?" I asked.

"Yes," she replied. "These people are a bunch of 'wannabees.' No one really gets it!"

"Gets what?" I responded.

"Gets the fact that we should not be focused on enjoyment in life but spiritual growth."

I questioned her back, "Is enjoyment not a part of spiritual growth? Should we not have balance of all things in our life? You are angry because people are not acting the way you would act. Have you reached perfection? You have called the people in the audience 'wannabes.' It seems you are upset because they are listening to all sides instead of 'wannabeing' like you!

"The higher power I believe in does not judge others and takes great pleasure in seeing all living beings embrace life, find happiness, and yes . . . even have fun! You must not believe you deserve to enjoy life," I concluded.

I was quite sure she would exit through the door without a word. To my surprise she said, "All this talk about balance. Every time something good happens to me, ten bad things follow. I just don't think it is meant for me to take pleasure from life. I feel like something awful will happen if I even laugh for a few seconds. In fact, it usually does."

She continued, "Please don't tell me all this stuff about me creating my own reality. I have heard it all, read it all, rented videotapes, audiotapes, and attended lectures and seminars!" Almost shouting she continued, "And yes, I paid attention, yes, I heard the words and understood, and yes, I prayed with intention!

"I quit eating meat to spiritually evolve more quickly. I gave up my daily glass of wine to practice discipline. I am at a job I am not happy with, as I know I am there to learn a lesson. What else can God want from me? And please, no sermons!"

I merely said, "Oh," and proceeded to walk away.

"Where are you going?" she said.

"I am going back inside to attend the remainder of the lecture," I answered.

She quickly growled, "No one has an answer for me!"

I responded, "Oh I have an answer, but I dare not share it with you, as you may not care for what I have to say."

"You're right," she said. "Don't bother. You will tell me I have been going through the motions of pursuing a spiritual path but am not really doing so."

"No," I gently replied.

In a frustrated voice she asked, "Okay, what do you think?"

I replied, "I think you should go eat a greasy cheeseburger, drink a glass of wine, look for a new job, and keep on praying!"

"What?" she exclaimed.

"You have forgotten to do things for yourself that made you happy. You are even afraid to laugh! Everything should be in moderation including spirituality. You have gone so far to the extreme of spirituality that you have taken a positive and created a negative."

I explained that she had tried to push her spiritual journey too quickly. The child just learning to play piano does not perform with the symphony orchestra until he learns to play properly. It's a slow process and takes time.

She finally broke a smile and almost laughed. "A cheeseburger does sound kind of good but I think I have given up on the power of prayer. I think prayers give people hope when all else fails but I really have my doubts these days."

I suggested she not give up and take my advice. She agreed that perhaps she was being too much of a spiritual martyr and would consider our conversation and give praying another try.

Many people including myself feel prayers are more than a plea to the Almighty. I think prayers can honestly produce miracles.

A double-blind study on the power of prayer was conducted by researchers at Kansas City's Mid-America Heart Institute at St. Luke's Hospital and published in *The Archives of Internal Medicine* in the late 1990s. It indicates that ill patients who were not aware that they were being prayed for or who was praying for them improved more rapidly over others.

This study was one of the largest to have taken place in this area of research. It addresses "remote intercessory prayer." The results validate that individuals showed signs of improved health when prayed for.

William Harris, Ph.D., a heart disease researcher led the study. After the admittance of 990 heart patients into St. Luke's Hospital Coronary Care Unit, 524 were randomly put into a control group. The remaining 466 patients were the individuals who were prayed for.

A prayer group of five volunteers prayed separately every day for these individuals for twenty-eight days after their admittance. The patients had no idea they were being prayed for nor did their physicians at the time.

The prayer groups were not told who they were praying for other than a first name. They did not have any details about any illnesses and only knew that the patients were hospitalized and not well. The patients had coronary heart disease, heart failure, and other cardiac conditions, some of which were life-threatening.

The conclusion was based on thirty-five different medical measurements. The length of time the patients stayed in the hospital was one form of measurement. Also, the use of pacemakers, medications, respirators and the length of time needed to use such applications was another consideration.

The results showed that the patients that were being prayed for did 11 percent better than the patients not being prayed for. Statistics indicate that the odds this could occur are approximately 1 in 27. These numbers are considered very meaningful in the realm of statistics.

Harris's research team included cardiologist James O'Keefe, the chaplain at St. Luke's Hospital, the Reverend Jerry Kolb, a statistician, other physicians, and a psychologist. James O'Keefe said, "I'll admit, being a scientist, I was very skeptical. There is no scientific mechanism to explain it. But from my perspective, I can tell you the message of this study is simple, clear, and harmless. If you or a

loved one are in trouble, medically ill, sick, and you feel so in-
clined, go ahead and pray. Pray for yourself and your loved ones.
This study suggests it might help."

This is not the first study to make this conclusion. In the late
1980s, Randolph Byrd, then a cardiologist at San Francisco General
Hospital, conducted what is considered to be the first serious research into the medical effects of intercessory prayer in a study of
393 heart patients. That study, too, showed a positive difference between patients who received intercessory prayer compared to con-
trols. Some estimated the difference at 10 percent.

One reason the Harris study is considered significant is that it is
the first since the Byrd study was published in a 1988 issue of *The
Southern Medical Journal* to try to duplicate the results.

That those were duplicated in a study that was better designed,
used 2½ times more patients, and was deemed solid enough to be
published in one of America's most respected medical journals is
believed, by some, to move the study of intercessory prayer and
health from pseudoscience and faith to one worthy of serious scientific consideration.

"This is a very well-designed study and it is very well-written,"
said James Dalen, editor of *The Archives of Internal Medicine* and
dean of the University of Arizona School of Medicine. "In this particular study, the patients benefited. If this was a medication, the
conclusion would be that this medication helped."

In the 1960s, at least two studies were conducted on the effects
of intercessory prayer. One involved eighteen children with leu-
kemia. The other involved forty-eight patients with various forms
of rheumatic illness. Both showed positive results. The patients
who were prayed for seemed to experience less overall illness. But
the studies were too small to be definitive.

Other larger studies are being conducted:

In Boston, Harvard University researcher Herbert Benson is
conducting a study on the effects of intercessory prayer on 1,800
patients admitted for heart surgery. The results of the study are expected late next year.

In Washington, D.C., physician Dale Matthews, an associate
professor of internal medicine at Georgetown University Medical
Center, reportedly is conducting a study on the effects of intercessory prayer on patients with a range of illnesses.

Last year, at the annual meeting of the American Heart Association, physician Mitchell Krucoff, an associate professor of medicine and cardiology at Duke University Medical Center, presented preliminary positive results of a study he is conducting on intercessory prayer involving 150 patients admitted to the hospital for cardiac catheterization.

"This is not fringe stuff anymore," Krucoff said. "This is now of mainstream scientific interest. I definitely think that the appearance of these types of studies in mainstream, peer-reviewed journals is a very exciting indication of where medicine is going in the new millennium."

More is known about the effects of personal prayer on health. Several studies in recent years have shown that patients who pray, or who simply possess deeply held spiritual beliefs, seem to heal faster and endure their illnesses with fewer complications compared with individuals who do not.

But studies of personal prayer are considered less controversial than studies of intercessory prayer. Whereas scientists say there are mechanisms to explain the positive effects of personal prayer—placebo effect, less stress, positive attitude, support from religious communities—there are no known mechanisms to explain why being prayed for by others may work.

For that reason, experts say, a lot more work needs to be done before doctors begin passing out prescriptions for prayer.

"It [the current study] does not offer irrefutable proof that this is a sure effect," Koenig said. "But it does offer evidence on which to build. It provides one more match on the stack of the evidence."

There are numerous stories about how the power of prayer has protected, cured, and positively changed people's lives. People of all civilizations and spiritual beliefs have prayers of some kind that they hold close to their hearts.

I have a special interest in prayers from all cultures, as well as what I call "old standards." I feel each has its own special influence. For that reason, I provide for you some prayers and thoughts that I hope you will find inspiring.

Prayers of Interest

Native American Lakota Chief Yellow Lark

Oh, Great Spirit,
whose voice I hear in the winds
and whose breath gives life to all the world, hear me.
I am small and weak.
I need your strength and wisdom.
Let me walk in beauty and make my eyes
ever behold the red and purple sunset.
Make my hands respect the things you have made
and my ears sharp to hear your voice.
Make me wise so that I may understand
the things you have taught my people.
Let me learn the lessons you have hidden
in every leaf and rock.
I seek strength, not to be superior to my brother,
but to fight my greatest enemy—myself.
Make me always ready to come to you
with clean hands and straight eyes,
so when life fades, as the fading sunset,
my spirit will come to you
without shame.

Chinese Philosopher Lao-tsu, Sixth Century B.C.

If there is to be peace in the world,
There must be peace in the nations.
If there is to be peace in the nations,
There must be peace in the cities.
If there is to be peace in the cities,
There must be peace between neighbors.
If there is to be peace between neighbors,
There must be peace in the home.
If there is to be peace in the home,
There must be peace in the heart.

African Tribal—Pygmy

In the beginning was God,
Today is God,
Tomorrow will be God.
Who can make an image of God?
He has no body.
He is the word which comes out of your mouth.
That word!
It is no more,
It is past, and still it lives!
So is God.

Psalm of David 61:1–4

Hear my cry, o God
listen to my prayer.
From the ends of the earth I call to you,
lead me to the rock that is higher than I.
For you have been my refuge,
a strong tower against the foe
I long to dwell in your tent forever
and take refuge in the shelter of your wings.

Irish, Bridgid of Gael, First Millennium

I arise today
Through a mighty strength
God's power to guide me,
God's might to uphold me,
God's eyes to watch over me,
God's ear to hear me,
God's word to give me speech,
God's hand to guard me,
God's way to lie before me,
God's shield to shelter me,
God's host to secure me.

Jesus of Nazareth, Matthew 7:7–8

Ask, and it shall be given you;
seek, and you shall find;
knock, and it shall be opened to you.
For whoever asks, receives;
and he who seeks, finds;
and to him who knocks, the door is opened.

'Abdu'l-Baha, Baha'i Prayers

O Thou kind Lord!
O Thou Who art generous and merciful!
We are servants of Thy threshold and are gathered
beneath the sheltering shadow of Thy divine unity.
The sun of Thy mercy is shining upon all,
and the clouds of Thy bounty shower upon all,
Thy gifts encompass all,
Thy loving providence sustains all,
Thy protection overshadows all,
and the glances of Thy favor are cast upon all.
O Lord! Grant Thine infinite bestowals,
and let the light of Thy guidance shine.
Illumine the eyes, gladden the hearts with abiding joy.
Confer a new spirit upon all people
and bestow upon them eternal life.
Unlock the gates of true understanding
and let the light of faith shine resplendent.
Gather all people beneath the shadow of Thy bounty
and cause them to unite in harmony,
so that they may become as the rays of one sun,
as the waves of one ocean,
and as the fruit of one tree.
May they drink from the same fountain.
May they be refreshed by the same breeze.
May they receive illumination from the same source of light
Thou art the Giver, the Merciful, the Omnipotent.

Messenger of Unity

You and I are One
All of You and Us are One.
All the Souls are One Soul
All the Lights are One Light.

Jesus, The Lord's Prayer, Matthew 6:9–13

Our Father which art in heaven,
Hallowed be thy name,
Thy kingdom come.
Thy will be done on earth,
as it is in heaven.
Give us this day our daily bread.
And forgive us our trespasses,
as we forgive those
who trespass against us.
And lead us not into temptation,
but deliver us from evil:
For thine is the kingdom,
and the power, and the glory,
forever and ever. Amen.

Angels and Prayer

I can hardly write a book on safeguarding people without including angels. Jane M. Howard writes in her book *Commune with
the Angels,* "The fact is that when you team up with the angels, they
add tremendous strength to your prayers. The idea is to allow
yourself to become partners in prayer with them. When you invoke the angels to pray with you, you call them forth from the an-
gelic realm to hear your request. Your invocation can be as simple
as, "In God's name, I invoke angels to add their power to my
prayers."

There are many ways in which to call angels. You may prefer to
say, "With the spirit of my higher power, I appeal to the angels to
assist me in my intentions." Sometimes lesser words are just as

powerful. You may simply choose to say, "Angels, help me send forth my prayers."

Angels have been considered protectors and guides since the beginning of time. While lecturing in Florida, one of the members of the audience shared with me how he was walking down the streets of a dangerous area in Indianapolis. What appeared to be a street gang was following him, closely behind. Alone and with no one in sight, he began to become fearful. "All I could think about was angels and light."

He visualized an angel holding a sword above his head and casting a white light around him that looked like a square. He continued to say, "This was fine, but I honestly was not convinced I was at all safe. Then I started to pray. The gang was getting closer as I could feel and hear them drawing nearer.

"Without warning flashing lights came from behind me. A police car pulled up and questioned the youths. The officers later drove up to me and warned me this was not a good area to walk at night and drove me back to my hotel."

He concluded by stating, "As I was in the squad car, I asked the officers if they believed in praying and angels. One commented, 'If I didn't, I doubt if I would still be here!' I told him he had discovered 'PAL.' 'What's "PAL?"' he said. 'PAL' is prayer, angels, and light."

Needless to say, always use common sense and take all physical precautions when necessary. PAL is not a way or a means of complete immunity from danger! Do not take foolish chances and uncalled-for risks.

Affirmations

Prayers are forceful and so are affirmations. Affirmations are spoken words or decrees. We do not have problems, just opportunities. Do not look at every fallback in life as a problem.

The Chinese describe the word "crisis" as "a dangerous opportunity." When we think about development and change, it may appear dangerous to us as this means giving up old ways and creating new ones. When you want something in life, however, change is unavoidable.

Plant the seed . . . the seed is thought. Think about your intention daily . . . this will water the seed. The seed now turns into habit. Habitual thinking grows into belief. Suddenly a sprout develops . . . the sprout is true belief. This belief will blossom into reality.

A good example of this is a conversation I heard years ago when traveling by bus. Two ladies where apparently on their way to an employment office. One was commenting to the other, "This place never finds work for anyone, I don't even know why I'm going." Naturally, the other woman wanted to know why and was told they were only interested in sign-up fees.

The seed was planted: "This place doesn't find people employment." If the lady thinks repeatedly about this thought, it will become something she now believes about this company. Before she is even called in for an interview, she has established a belief that she will not find work from this firm.

A way to guard yourself from being influenced by other people's experiences is affirmations. Through repetition of a particular thought, we create a habit. Our habit becomes belief and that belief becomes truth. Remember, thought . . . habit . . . belief. I have always said, "If I can think it, I can do it."

Affirmations do not have to be pages of words and decrees. Let me suggest a few affirmations to recite every morning and evening.

Think about what it is you are trying to achieve—only one thought. "I want a new job, a boyfriend, and a new car" will not work. That is being greedy and overloading your brain. Focus on something really special, e.g., "I see my health improving."

Sit quietly on a chair and close your eyes. Repeat five times, "I see myself [fill in what you are in search of]." Do not say, "I want" or "I need"! If you say, "I want," you will always want; if you say "I need," you will always need. Always say, "I see myself."

After you have repeated your affirmation five times, be still for a minute or so and visualize the final outcome. Don't worry about how it will transpire; just see the end result. If you want to lose thirty pounds, see the scale reading thirty pounds lighter. Do not see yourself signing up for a diet program or running ten miles a day. The universe will find the way to provide the results you desire. Just keep your focus on the final goal. This will start the process of change in your life. Do this twice a day.

Do not just say the words but think about what you are saying. Arnold Schwarzenegger once said, regarding bodybuilding, "One repetition with intention is worth ten without." This applies to all things in life.

Above all, remember to be patient. A friend of mine once put it nicely by saying, "You don't dig up a seed to see how it is growing!"

Affirmations are about positive changes in your life in all distinct areas. I have included a few that are uplifting. Create your own or make changes to the ones I provide to suit your needs. Keep in mind to sit quietly, close your eyes, and be calm when reciting your affirmations.

- I know all things happen for a higher purpose. There are no mistakes. Therefore, I do not worry. Everything is in my best interest and I am truly blessed.

- My experiences can never be too good. My life is joyous and prosperous. I live in amazing grace.

- Today I choose all that is positive, protective, and peaceful. My life is changing for the better.

- I go within myself and hear the voice of the Divine. I will listen to the message and be receptive. Thank you for your guidance.

- I am a creative individual and will use my gifts to bring forth joy and happiness into my life and the lives of others. I am safeguarded from forces that will not allow me to create. I am successful. And so it is.

- I release all dependency that has inflicted my life. I forgive; I take responsibility. I have changed and have grown to a higher level or understanding. God walks with me. I am never alone.

- I no longer wait for my ship to come into port. I swim out to it and sail it in myself. I am determined.

- I remind myself today that I will not wish, hope, or pray for anything. I will not contemplate or visualize what I require. I will "just be" in the sparkling light of all existence. I am.

- Today, my heart is without fear. God is my partner. We will cocreate together.

- All is available to me in life. I now believe in myself and know I can do anything, as long as it comes through love. It's so simple . . . so simple. I believe.

CHAPTER 10

Rituals and Ceremonies

There is a very slight technical difference between a ritual and a ceremony. In fact, they are still typically categorized as the same. The two words have become comingled. The dictionary describes a ritual as a ceremony, and a ceremony as a ritual. They are basically synonyms. Yet, if you investigate further, you will also find that definitions describe rituals as repeated rites and do not necessarily say the same about ceremonies.

For instance, Ancient Greeks and Romans had yearly rituals honoring gods or goddesses. All cultures around the world have rituals they perform at a given time. Some stem from religious observances, the welcoming of a season or yearly festivals. Whether in North America, Australia, Asia, Russia, Europe, Africa, or South America, rituals are a part of all civilizations.

Ceremonies are usually experienced by more than one person. Often dancing, singing, and all-around celebration are included as a part of these affairs. Often a ritual becomes a ceremony.

The following rituals and ceremonies are some of the best I have found for defense against negative energies and clearing homes and business of lingering opposing influences. They provide a way of releasing trapped negativity and inviting positive luck and fortune into our lives.

Smudging Ritual for Protection and Purification

Smudging or "sweeping the smoke" is a Native American custom using sacred herbs and plants such as sage, cedar, or sweetgrass to perform cleansing rituals. We can smudge a place for protection and to rid it of unwanted forces. We can also smudge people to ward off sickness, as well as remove negative vibrations from them.

Anything that you feel needs new vitality can be smudged. When moving into a new house or dwelling, I recommend smudging. At the office, smudge your work area if possible. It may be difficult to achieve without anyone noticing, but well worth it if you can find a time when no one is present.

I smudge my computer now and then when I feel my creative talents are stagnant. I know an artist who smudges his brushes and canvas before starting a new project. It is a way of clearing the old energy and allowing the new to flow through.

A massage therapist, who traveled regularly with his wife, shared with me the fact that he would smudge their cat every time it came back from staying with his mother-in-law! He claimed he could feel his mother-in-law's energy permeating from the cat and it made him very frustrated. Once the cat was smudged, all was peaceful again.

To a smudge a person, place, animal, or object, you need only a few things:

- A white sage stick or loose sage. If using loose sage, you will need a bowl or seashell to hold it and a fan or feather in order to help spread the smoke.

- A charcoal lighter or candle.

Other herbs and plants such as cedar or sweetgrass can be used, but white sage is the most readily available and is excellent for smudging. The reason white sage is preferred is that it is a powerful medicine. Native Americans burn it as protection against hostile energies. It sets a type of boundary that evil forces and negativity cannot cross. Sage is an all-around form of purification.

It can be purchased loose or bought in a bundle, usually wrapped with cotton yarn. The wrapped bundle is referred to as a smudge stick.

White sage smudge sticks or loose sage can usually be found in Native American stores, New Age gift shops, or some health food and herbal stores. These are not costly items. If buying loose white sage, it will be in the form of dried leaves.

Through the years I have found the smudge stick the easiest to use. However, if you choose to use loose sage, you must put it in a bowl or use a large seashell if available. A shell represents water, which is a purifier.

If using a seashell, put sand on the bottom of it or use something like a pot holder or cloth so as to not burn yourself from the heat.

Loose sage will require you to use a fan or feather to move the smoke around, as you cannot hold it in your hand and wave it, like a sage stick. Of course, you can always use your hands to disperse the smoke if you do not have a fan or feather. Experiment with both techniques and see which you prefer.

Whether loose sage or a bundle, you will need a long charcoal lighter. A match or regular lighter will not work as it takes a while for the sage to light. Some people prefer using a candle to light the herbs, as you do not have to keep clicking it as you may with a lighter.

Before you begin this ritual, always say out loud or to yourself your intention and the reason for smudging. For instance: I smudge this home for the protection and safekeeping of all who dwell here; I smudge Mary to dispel the negativity that has befallen her; I smudge my cat Sylvester so he will be safe while prowling in the neighborhood; I smudge Ben so he will be cleared of his ill health; I smudge my office to cleanse it of restricted energy so my finances will improve.

Smudging an individual can be performed outside or inside. If using loose sage, take your bowl or shell that contains the sage and light it. Be patient as it takes a while for the embers to start to smolder. Once they do, take the bowl in one hand and the feather or fan in the other. Starting at the feet of the person to be smudged, fan the smoke around them, not allowing it to blow into their eyes.

The reason you smudge from their feet up is because smoke

rises. When you reach their head, flick the feather or use your hand as a way to disperse negativity from their aura. Be sure to smudge both the back and the front of the person.

When using a sage stick to smudge an individual, you can light the sage in the same fashion and wave it back and forth in front of them from their toes to their head. Flick the energy away with your hand as above.

You can also smudge yourself if you are doing things solitary. If using loose white sage, light the sage and place the bowl on the floor or ground. Stand and turn in a circle in front of it, allowing the smoke to rise around you. Another method that works well is to wave your smudge stick or bowl of sage in the air and walk through the smoke. Do this a few times until you feel you have achieved your purpose.

When smudging the interior or exterior of a building or abode, you must first smudge all those who are present for this ritual. Once you have done this, make certain that someone, in turn, smudges you or you smudge yourself.

Once all participants have been cleared of any stagnant or negative energy, you can proceed to smudge the dwelling. If possible, open the windows. This provides circulation for the air, as you want it to renew.

Start at the front door and in a clockwise motion go from room to room. Use your feather, fan, or hand to direct the smoke. If using a smudge stick, direct it accordingly and make sure the smoke drifts into the corners of every room.

Do not forget to smudge the closets, laundry room, or any storage areas as well. Do not create too much smoke. If you should start to become irritated by the smoke, you have probably lit too much sage.

If at any time your sage burns out, relight it and continue from where you stopped. When you have completed the process, you should find yourself back at the front door where you started.

Put out your sage in any manner and save the remainder for another time. This ritual should allow you to sense almost immediately a more positive energy in the location. Colors will be more vivid and there will be a new zest in the area. The place should feel enlivened and fresh.

To smudge an object, such as a desk, use the same technique

and do the best you can to pass smoke around it. You can smudge a table full of items as opposed to each one individually. Smudging can also be used for protection of a vehicle, bicycle, or any form of transportation.

Smudging is an exciting and calming ritualistic way of clearing unwanted energy. Perform a smudging ritual whenever you feel it needs to be done. Use your intuition. Remember that this is not a cure for sickness or catastrophic events. It is a mind, body, and soul connection that I have seen make powerful transformations in individuals' lives.

I once suggested to a friend of mine, who was not doing well in her business life, that she should allow me to carry out this smudging ritual. Although she was a bit of a skeptic, she was also a good sport and allowed me to conduct this rite on my balcony.

It was not necessary for her to be at her own home as she was the one who was getting smudged. As I lit my white sage stick, I thought in silence, "May the energy that is stopping her from success be discarded and replaced with new enthusiasm and the liveliness of prosperity." Within one week she secured a new job with three times the money she was previously earning. Her social life also took on an added lift! Needless to say, she has now purchased her own smudge stick and conducts this ceremony when she feels it is necessary! (See Chapter 20: "Name Utilization Ceremonies," for blessings using sage.)

The Orange Peel Blessing Ceremony

This Chinese ceremony adjusts the ch'i (energy) and serves as a safeguard against problems, chaotic behavior, ill health, and loss of any kind. This blessing is performed in the interior of a home or building. Its purpose is to bless the inhabitants and to alleviate unexplained energies that are disruptive to the occupants.

This ceremony uses the influence of the orange, which is uplifting and works to energize us and the building to which we are applying this method. I have heard many different ways to conduct the Orange Peel Blessing and have been told that there is no exact right or wrong way of carrying out this ceremony. If you adhere to the basics, it will work.

Items you will need:

- Nine oranges.

- A large mixing bowl.

- Freshly cut flowers from a florist, a grocery store, or your own garden. The flowers should not be purchased or picked for any other reason than to conduct this ceremony.

Once you have gathered all your items, follow these steps:

- Perform a mudra, which is a spiritual hand gesture that has special meaning to you. It can be in the form of praying hands. Placing both palms together with fingers pointing up. You may also choose a heart-calming mudra. This is where you place your left hand on top of the right hand with your palms facing up and the tips of your thumbs touching each other.

- Another alternative is to simply hold your hands in front of you, somewhat cupped with your palms up, in a receiving gesture.

- While your hands are still in position, chant a mantra (sacred words of power), prayer, or chant that means something sacred to you. Repeat it nine times. For example: Hail Mary full of grace . . . or, May my higher power protect this dwelling from ill fate . . . etc.

- Fill the bowl with water approximately three-fourths full.

- Peel the nine oranges and tear the peels into small pieces. You do not need the rest of the oranges.

- Place the peels in your bowl of water.

- Take your bowl of oranges and water to the front door. With a mild flicking action using your thumb, ring, and middle fingers, sprinkle the doorway as you pass through. Think about the reason that you are performing this ceremony and what you hope to achieve.

Then, walk through the house or building in the direction your intuition guides you, and sprinkle all the rooms and any spe-

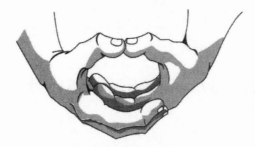

The Orange Peel Blessing: Heart-Calming Mudra

cial areas where you may pick up negative "vibes." As you walk and scatter your orange water, periodically or constantly recite your mantra, prayer, or chant.

You need not use all of the water. Also, be careful of furnishings or other items that should not be in contact with water. When you are finished, you can dispose of the rest of the water and orange peels.

- Next, place your flowers in a location that is centrally located and has a place of dignity.

- If possible, open your front door and as many windows as feasible. Keep the doors and windows open for at least fifteen minutes. This symbolically blows the unfavorable energy out and allows favorable energy to enter. If you cannot open the door or windows completely for fifteen minutes, open a window as much as possible for a few minutes. If all else fails, open the door and visualize the unwanted energy leaving in seconds and then see the positive flowing through and shut the door immediately.

- Take care of your flowers and replace the water often. When they begin to wilt, throw them out or replace them with new ones.

CHAPTER 11

Gemstones and Herbs

Specific gemstones and herbs have special influences that can assist in your psychic fortification and self-defense methods. Throughout time, we have been intrigued and enchanted with gemstones. It is not only their beauty that fascinates us but also the "feeling" we receive when we wear a special stone. All gemstones have a different frequency. Some promote healing while others may promote love or protection.

However, I must draw special attention to clear quartz crystals, which are one of the most powerful of gemstones. They bring life to our quartz watches. They receive and transmit radio waves. Without quartz crystals, the computer age would never have happened: they are what make up integrated circuits and electronic chips.

But the power of crystals goes far beyond the products we have derived from them. They are important tools in psychic self-defense, with the ability to focus and direct energy to a specific intention.

Also, keep in mind that a clear quartz crystal will always help intensify the power of any other gemstones with which it is used.

Gemstones Used for Defense and Guardianship

All the following gemstones can be worn as a form of jewelry, set in a specific location in your office or home, carried with you in a variety of ways, or used in rituals and ceremonies to further influence the objective of the rite.

Clear quartz crystal. Stimulates healing, balances the elements to fulfill us, and make us whole. Guards us from psychic aggression from the living and the nonliving.

Amethyst. Its curative properties have been used by psychics and healers for years. Helpful in dispelling anger and anxiety, aids in feeling less scattered.

Bloodstone. Encourages caution. Insulates us from stress and anxiety.

Chalcedony. Dismisses nightmares, and prevents one from becoming irritable.

Red coral. Acts like a shield from harm. Some ancient civilizations thought those who wore coral could calm violent storms and stay safe.

Fire agate. Creates a feeling of security and safety. It is a calming stone.

Jet. Said to combat manic-depressive behavior. It has balancing qualities that keep one focused on taking care of oneself.

Obsidian. Keeps away negativity of all types. It is a highly protective and masculine stone. It absorbs stress-related psychic aggression emanating from other people.

Pyrite. Soothes anxiety and protects the skin from the elements. Safeguards one in groups of people.

Sard. Worn as protection against evil spells and black magic.

Lapis lazuli.   Draws love to us and guards our health. It is also reputed to be effective in healing headaches, high blood pressure, depression, insomnia, and other such ailments.

Malachite.   Increases energy, and is connected to change and creativeness. The Egyptians wore crushed malachite as eye shadow to guard against the evil eye.

Turquoise.   Builds strength. It is the sacred stone to the Native Americans. It is a protective stone for horses and their riders. It has the quality of absorbing negative energy directed at an individual.

Gemstones you program for protection will deflect negative energy that is headed your way. Whether these stones are polished or raw stone should not make a difference. There are those, however, who feel the unpolished raw stones are more connected to the earth and carry stronger vibrations, as they have not been put through a tumbling process. Judge for yourself and go with the stone that draws you.

Keep in mind that the stone chooses you; you do not pick the stone. It will just "feel good" in your hand.

Once you find your gemstone, it needs to be cleared, charged, and programmed for psychic defense. I have found that some individuals only clear, charge, and program clear quartz crystals, but I believe all gemstones should go through this process.

You start by cleansing it of the energy of other people who may have handled your stone. This also applies to jewelry containing gemstones as well.

There are many methods with which to clear a gemstone. Here is one that is very successful.

Wash the stone in cold water and than let it sit in a bowl of water for twenty-four hours. Some people put salt in the water to aid in purifying it. If you are fortunate enough to live near an ocean or body of salt water, take your gemstone to the water and submerge it a few times. Imagine you are washing off all the energy of anyone who has previously come in contact with this stone.

I recommend putting the stone in a mesh bag or cheesecloth before immersing it, so it does not drift into the sea. You can clear more than one item at a time if you like.

After you have cleansed your gemstone, you should charge it.

Charging a gemstone means stimulating or refreshing its natural ability to direct energy. Again, there are many methods to accomplish this. You can set your gemstone in the sunlight for several hours or leave it overnight under a full or new moon. A full moon as always is the most powerful phase. A new moon is a time for growth, new beginnings, and optimism. The solar power of the sun rushes into the gemstone and energizes it with renewal, courage, warmth, and brightness.

Once you have cleared and charged your gemstone, the last step is to program it. Hold it in your hand, examine the stone carefully, and get in touch with it. Focus on the vibration of protection that the stone generates. You may want to say a few words like, "Keep me free from harm," "Keep negativity out of my life," or just "Protection."

There might be something in particular from which you need to be safeguarded. If this is the case, focus on that goal. See yourself calm, safe, and free from psychic attack.

A good way to protect your home is to program a quartz cluster or amethyst cluster and display it in a prominent area. I also suggest planting clear quartz crystals in a circle around your house. Program several small stones as above for protection and bury them around the perimeter of your house in a clockwise direction. A circle is a powerful and influential symbol. When it comes to protection, nothing penetrates the circle.

If you live in a condominium or apartment, you can put crystals around your home, a few in each room on all sides of the entire unit. Visualize all the crystals connected by a line that would form a circle. Utilize windowsills; place them under rugs, on tables, or wherever it is workable.

Charging Water for Safekeeping Your Health

To safeguard your health, try charging your drinking water. This technique will energize you, and protect your body from energy drain.

To charge your water, use a clear glass pitcher or container of some kind. Pour distilled or spring water into your container.

Select one or more of the gemstones that promote protection, such as amethyst or clear quartz crystals. Make sure you have cleared the gemstones that you have chosen, and that they are clean.

In this particular case you are tapping into the generic influences the stones carry, so it is up to you whether you program it or not. Next, drop your stones into the water.

Place your hands with the palms down above your container. In a circular clockwise motion, pass your hands over the top of the container. This is a way of changing the water to match the properties of the stone. If possible, place the water in the sun for a few hours. When you drink the water, the protective influences of the stones will affect your body in a positive manner.

Drink the water when you feel you need it. I do not refrigerate mine, but many people prefer it. If you make a large amount and will not use it all immediately, make sure you have a cover for the container. Use caution—remove gemstones before drinking.

If you are sensitive, you should be able to taste the difference between charged water and water that is not charged. Do your own experiment at home. Have friends come over and do not let them know which is which. See if they can tell the difference. Usually, the majority will be able to guess the charged water!

Herbs

Herbs also have protective properties. Throughout history the use of herbs has been documented for many diverse purposes. They are used for enhancing our food, healing, spiritual attunement, and aromatic affects. Herbs are hung over doorways, employed in ceremonies, made into essential oils, used for dream pillows, and that's just a few of the uses.

A dream pillow is a fantastic way to guard yourself against nightmares and insomnia. As I dream lucidly, I have almost total control of my dreams and can change them at will even in the dream state if something frightens me.

However, when I heard about dream pillows, I sought out friends, clients, family members, and anyone who would help me with the dream pillow experiment. These people had one thing in common: they couldn't sleep well at night and were jumpy or suffered from nightmares. I had a dream pillow party and invited a group over to make the pillows.

Everyone reported back that since they have used their dream pillows, they have had no nightmares or difficulty sleeping! It was difficult for me to believe that not even one felt it did not work. I believe in conducting my own research in addition to those of others and the dream pillows seem to free people from nightmares and insomnia. I know the healing effects of herbs on all levels—body, mind, and soul—so why was I so surprised?

You can purchase dream pillows with a variety of different herbs for different reasons, although I think no one can make anything as powerful as what you can make for yourself. This is not to say dream pillows made by other people cannot be programmed for your intention—they certainly can. When purchasing a dream pillow from someone else, try to find a source that is sincere and makes the pillows with love and good intentions. In fact, most people who deal with herbs and oils not only are creative but also want to help others by the use of what nature has given us. What better intention can there be?

Dream pillows use both herbs and essential oils. Please note the difference between them.

In the text *Essential Oils Desk Reference*, compiled by Essential Science Publishing, essential oils are described as follows:

Subtle, volatile liquids distilled from shrubs, flowers, trees, roots, bushes, and seeds. They are highly concentrated and far more potent than dried herbs. The distillation of an entire plant may produce only a single drop of essential oil. Essential oils are also different from vegetable oils, such as corn oil, peanut oil, and olive oil. They are not greasy and do not clog the pores like vegetable oils can.

The *Essential Oils Desk Reference* goes on to say:

Hieroglyphics on the walls of Egyptian temples depict the blending of oils and describe hundreds of oil recipes.

A sacred room in the temple of Isis on the island of Philae depicts a ritual called "Cleansing the Flesh and Blood of Evil Deities." This emotional clearing required three days of cleansing using essential oils.

Romans purified their temples and political buildings by diffusing essential oils. They also used aromatics in their steam baths to both invigorate the flesh and ward off disease.

How to Create a Dream Pillow to Repel Nightmares and Insomnia

Items you will need to create your dream pillow:

Herbs for protection and to dispel nightmares
Pick out some herbs from the list provided. They can be purchased from an herbalist or health food store.

Bay laurel
Blackberry
Cedar
Cinnamon
Frankincense
Mugwort
Mullein
Sandalwood
St. John's wort
Thyme

Essential oils
Lavender
Jasmine
Hyacinth
Bergamot
Marjoram
Valerian

An eyedropper

A bowl
This should be glass or wood. *Do not use metal.*

Fabric
Two pieces of plain cloth, each 8 by 12 inches. Muslin works
nicely.
Two pieces of decorative fabric, each also 8 by 12 inches.

Something you find soothing or attractive. Check out your local fabric store and see what makes you feel peaceful and calm. It can be a print or a solid color.

How to sew and fill your dream pillow:

Take your two pieces of plain cloth or muslin and turn the fabric inside out. Stitch or sew the 8-inch sides together (on the wrong side) and then sew one 12-inch side together. The stitching should be about ¾ inch into the fabric. You should have three sides sewn together and a 12-inch side still open. Turn the bag right side out. This is the part of the pillow that will hold your herbal blend.

Next, using your better fabric, sew as above. Only this time do not make the bag as small. Sew closer to the edges. Remember that the plain bag holding the herbs must fit inside the second bag.

You can choose to make the outer cover washable by attaching Velcro or snaps to the open end.

Take your selected herbs and mix them in your glass or wooden bowl. Do not mix aggressively. Be gentle. You can actually toss the herbs if you wish. As you are mixing these ingredients, remember the intention of this pillow.

Fill your eyedropper with the oils you have chosen. Slowly add a drop at a time to the herb mix. Do not use more than five drops. When you sleep on the pillow and the aroma is right next to you, it is far stronger than what you will smell from a foot away.

Fill your inner pillow with the herbal combination. Use just enough to fill the bag but do not make it bulge. In other words, it should be a bit on the flat side. Turn the open part of the fabric to make a hem and sew it up. Insert it in your larger pillow and either sew it together completely or close it using Velcro or snaps.

You are now ready to use your dream pillow.

Some people set it on their regular pillow and sleep on top of it. I have also heard many individuals slip it in the pillowcase of their regular pillow, thus having it covered by the pillowcase yet not losing the comfort of a standard pillow. Try a few different routines and enjoy a good night's sleep!

CHAPTER 12

Symbols, Charms, Amulets, and Talismans

Symbols are what fairy tales are made of: mythology, history, religion, literature, archeology, and art. We encounter symbols every day in our lives and they can be very powerful. These icons serve as reminders and protectors and create wonderment and curiosity about their origin.

Symbolic images can move our thoughts and elevate our awareness. Contemplation, introspection, and meditation can be enhanced by the utilization of these fascinating representations. They enrich our understanding of things not always in the physical world. Ancient civilizations and cultures utilized these emblems daily.

Often I ask myself, how is it some cultures from opposites ends of the planet had the same meanings for the same symbol and yet others had contrasting interpretations?

We wear symbols in jewelry, charms, talismans, or amulets. We place them in temples, churches, pyramids, and works of art.

As we travel through the twenty-first century, I still see much symbolism but it is more in the form of icons on computers or used in advertising a product. Traffic signs and airport signs are pictorial and symbolic. Symbols are all around us but in a different form. These modern-day symbols do not have their own personal, magical, or artistic appeal.

It is very doubtful an artist will paint on a cathedral wall the symbol of a circle with a slanted line drawn through it and a cigarette with smoke fuming out the end. However, you may find one on a plastic sign in the lobby! These are symbols we must learn in order to deal with everyday life.

I have great respect for the symbolism of days gone by, not only for their creative level but the meanings behind them and the beliefs our ancestors put into them. I think we should start paying more attention to the symbolism of the past and put it to use in the present.

A symbol on a piece of jewelry, painting, or sculpture or a statue of a special figure that represents something particular to you may bring back a bit of hope and appeal to your subconscious mind. It will remind you that we do have the ability to manipulate our thoughts and eventually alter situations in life for the better.

The purpose of this section is to acquaint you with a few symbols typically used for protection on some level throughout history.

More people believe in the use of symbols than we may realize. An audience member at a lecture I was giving came to me very quietly afterward and said she could appreciate the history behind symbology but she did not believe in it on any level. She proceeded to say she thought it was all superstition promoting false hope and that symbols did no good and had no meaning that would inform or educate. She felt they had no true value.

I said to her, "You are a very lovely woman, I imagine men are inviting you out all the time." "No!" she exclaimed. "They could see from my wedding ring that I am a married woman!" With the raise of an eyebrow, I smiled and said nothing, but she heard the message loud and clear!

Decide for yourself what you believe and don't. However, I hope this section of the book will stimulate you to explore further the symbols to which you are drawn. If you are drawn to something, it is usually because of a special message that can be of benefit to you.

Symbols for Protection

Charms and Amulets

Usually worn on the body, especially around the neck, to dispel evil or to protect the wearer from injury.

Talisman

An object marked with significant symbols or cast with positive thoughts that can have a strong power of protection is a talisman. It also can bestow on its bearer abilities beyond the physical.

A talisman must be programmed for a specific purpose by a person strong of mind and with a strong belief of things that are not of the physical plane. A talisman can be cast for protection, luck, love, or anything one so chooses.

I have taken many medallions, crystals, and pieces of jewelry and turned them into what one would describe as a magical talisman.

Here is a quick method you may want to experiment with to cast a talisman. As this book is about psychic protection, I will use this topic as the intention. However, you can use this method for love, luck, prosperity, or anything that is positive.

You cannot cast a talisman to cause harm to its wearer or for ill purposes. If you do, it will come back to you three times three in a very dismal manner. Have fun in invoking this ritual. The magic is all up to you and what you believe.

How to Cast a Talisman Take a medallion, charm, or anything that can be put onto a chain or string and worn around the neck. You may want to use a crystal, cross, pentagram, or any symbol that means something to you or the person who will be receiving it. The talisman does not have to be in necklace form, but when it comes in contact with your body, it is more powerful. A ring or bracelet would work as well. Or you can always carry something in your wallet or purse that you keep near to you. It can be something inexpensive or worth a thousand dollars. Energy and magic know no price. The value stems from the aim of the person performing this practice.

- On the night of a full moon, wash your charm with cold water and see it becoming clear of all energies that were previously put on it by others or by yourself. Dry it with a clean white cloth of paper towel.

- Place it out in full view of the moon (outside if possible).

If you cannot use the outdoors, put it in front of a window or door that looks outside. If this is totally impossible and you have no window, draw a picture of a full moon and place it on the picture. No matter where it is placed, the moon eventually passes over that area so do not go to any lengths for the perfect spot.

- Once the trinket is in place, throw a bit of salt on the piece and say:

  This once an ordinary charm
  Now keep me safe from fear and harm.
  And so it is.

- Leave it in its position for twenty-four hours.

- Remove the salt and clean it a bit. Wear it when you feel the need for protection.

If indeed your intention was strong, you have taken an ordinary piece of jewelry and created a talisman!

The Cross

This symbol represents universal protection, whether displayed in a home, worn as a necklace, or incorporated with other symbolic forms. People hang them above doorways to keep evil from entering and display them in automobiles to protect themselves while driving.

Crosses were drawn on shields and carried into battle as a symbolic defense. There are many types of crosses from all different cultures. We see multitudes of sizes and shapes adorning churches, cathedrals, and religious artwork.

The fact that it is made up of the vertical crossing the horizontal is very interesting. From a duality we create a whole.

It also divides an area into four sections, a crossroads. It is said that in certain African civilizations the people were advised to pass through crossroads as often as possible because it confuses imposing spirits who are following someone as to which way to continue. A cross of any type is always a dignified and acceptable symbol of protection that is universally understood.

Pentagram

This is a most highly misunderstood symbol. Somehow Hollywood and fantasy filmmakers often show this as a Satanic emblem. This is not the case.

The symbol normally is used in an upright position, in which case it is an ancient symbol of protection from evil. When inverted, it is often associated with negative forces. Just as a cross right side up is considered to be a positive symbol, if it is depicted upside down, what is the reaction?

The pentagram is typically drawn as a five-pointed star with all five lines connecting. Sometimes it is shown with a circle encompassing it, which represents wholeness and completion. When the circle is included, it is called a pentacle (see figure). To some, the lowest four points represent the elements of earth, air, fire, and water. The topmost point is also said to be considered the fifth element—spirit. This representation suggests that the spiritual world has command over the material world.

Another interpretation is that when drawn in the upright position, the pentagram can easily represent the human body. This indicates the pentagram as the star of the macrocosm, or small universe. This interpretation suggests that within ourselves we are a small universe. We contain all that the greater universe contains.

Pentacle

The pentagram can be worn in any form of jewelry. We see it displayed on objects of all types and often carved in wooden doors and gates. It is used in magic rituals as a form of protection while the ritual is under way.

In certain circumstances, when I know and am apprehensive about a situation, I wear a well-hidden pentagram necklace hanging down my back as opposed to my chest. In this way "my back is covered" from any interference I do not want to encounter.

Bells

These are used in religious ceremonies, as a musical instrument and as a means to dispel evil forces. Bells are positive symbols of defense. Bells drive away evil spirits and ward off storms. In France bells were rung to avert lightning.

Circle

This is one of the most significant symbols and the most prevalent of all geometric shapes. There is no beginning and no end to a circle. It symbolizes universal oneness. In rituals and ceremonies a circle is sometimes cast or drawn to protect the person conducting the ritual. Everything is safe within the circle.

Saint Christopher

Considered the patron saint of travelers. Many people wear Saint Christopher in the form of an amulet to protect them from sudden death. Also, you will see small Saint Christopher statues in cars or trucks.

Peacock

A bird of protection and of guardianship. Native Americans used peacock feathers in fans and in many of their crafts as they were thought of as positive influences. The Chinese view peacocks with the utmost respect as they represent beauty and majestic qualities. In India gods are illustrated riding on or accompanied by these fine birds. Folklore tells us a peacock feather in the home protects the positive energy within. It emanates serenity and harmony.

Dragon

In Chinese philosophy, the dragon is used in forms of decorating to ward off evil and is considered a representation promoting happiness and well-being. Also in China there is a dragon boat festival held the first full moon of April every year. This festival is said to please the dragons, which the Chinese feel are of great protective value to their communities. Conversely, in Christianity the dragon can represent Satanic elements that Michael the archangel defeated. This is why dragons are often depicted with flames of fire spewing from their mouths. As one belief system recognizes the dragon as a protector and another as a creature with a negative aspect, whether to use a dragon symbol as a form of protection depends on what your doctrines are.

Tiger

Tigers' heads are often seen on doorknockers. This is more than a mere decorative piece for the entrance. It is said that demons fear tigers and hence defend your abode. Tigers were also set on gravestones in China to keep away evil spirits.

Udjat Eye

This symbol has been found on amulets from ancient Egypt. It is also referred to as the Eye of Horus. It is depicted as a human eye and eyebrow (see figure). When worn as an amulet, it was usually

The Udjat Eye

created from a blue or green semiprecious stone. This symbol was worn as a means of preventing sickness.

Anchor

Symbolizing security and safety, an anchor prevents us from becoming unstable. This emblem also symbolizes hope and confidence. It protects us from drifting the wrong way in life.

Be sure to research all symbols you have no knowledge of before utilizing them or bringing them into your home. They have powerful energies and can work for or against you!

CHAPTER 13

Feng Shui

Feng Shui (pronounced "fung shway") is an Ancient Chinese art, science, and philosophy. Every aspect of your life can be improved through this practice of harmonizing your environment and energy flow. As I mentioned earlier, this energy flow is referred to by the Chinese as ch'i. There is good positive ch'i or bad negative ch'i. In the Western world, in the seventies, we would use the word "vibes" to describe such an energy force. "This place has 'bad vibes!'" or "She's sending me 'good vibes.'"

As you can feel ch'i, you can also direct it to flow in a more positive and protective manner.

Very simply put, by the placement of furniture or adding or removing certain objects in your home or workplace, you can change the flow of ch'i. When the flow of ch'i is balanced, you can shift luck, prosperity, romance, health, and creativity to enrich your life.

As this book is about how to protect yourself from negative influences, I will focus on the area of Feng Shui that deals with protection. However, the entire art of Feng Shui is most fascinating.

I personally utilize Feng Shui and recommend you look further into the subject. Feng Shui has had a great impact on my life, as well as millions of others. Donald Trump is one of the many well-known business tycoons who consults a Feng Shui expert to advise him before any real estate transactions are considered.

Feng Shui is a complex Chinese science and should be approached with seriousness. Some concepts of Feng Shui used in the

Western world have been very distorted. Hence, if you decide to get a better understanding of these principles, look to professional and authentic sources.

One of the main instrumental elements of Feng Shui is using the ba-gua (pronounced "bah-gwah"). Some refer to it as the Feng Shui octagon. The ba-gua is an octagonal symbol of the *I Ching*, which is an ancient text of divination that offers guidance.

The *I Ching* triagrams link nature and humanity to each other. The ba-gua can be superimposed on a layout of a home or building to determine the energetic environment that affects the residents. By using the ba-gua, a Feng Shui practitioner will divide a space into nine sections, each having its own influences. The areas are: helpful people, career, knowledge, family, wealth, fame, relationship, children/creativity, and health.

Once he (or she) has seen what furnishings and structural area he is dealing with, the consultant will offer cures to resolve uneasiness in the individual's lifestyle. For instance, if you have a broken lamp in your wealth area, your finances may be in trouble. The Feng Shui practitioner will tell you to remove the lamp and offer suggestions as to how to place your furniture in the room to promote more wealth.

If you have a neighbor who is a nuisance, the Feng Shui practitioner will also explain how to protect yourself from the ch'i of your neighbor that comes your way, by the placement of special items or ceremonies.

With a bit of study and guidance, you can be your own Feng Shui practitioner and protect your own environment.

Color use, elements, objects representing a special intention, and blessings are all a part of Feng Shui.

Colors

Red: protection, power, movement.
Green: growth, hope, new beginnings.
Blue: knowledge, sky.
Purple: wealth, energy.
Pink: romance, parenthood, love.
Yellow: health, longevity.
White: purity. (The Chinese wear white when mourning the departed.) Like black, too much white should be avoided.

Black: admiration, power. (Black should not be overdone, as it
will represent loss if taken to an extreme.)

Below I offer you some Feng Shui practices that promote protection. Please remember, to present detailed information about
this ancient art in this small part of the book would be impossible.
I furnish this section as a way to casually introduce you to this ancient science and hope you would pursue it more extensively on
your own.

When correcting an area using Feng Shui, the uses and placements of objects or intentions are referred to as cures or remedies.
When applying a cure, you should think about what it is you are
trying to achieve while you are carrying out the process. Intention
is the greatest cure.

A Few Feng Shui Cures

Bamboo flutes have many meanings in Feng Shui and can be
used for a multitude of reasons. Bamboo flutes were important in
history, as they were used to deliver good news and to inform residents that all was safe on a given day. Therefore, in Feng Shui they
represent safety and peace. They are also considered protective
and are said to drive away misfortune.

The flutes or flute should be hung horizontally in areas you intuitively feel need protection. Perhaps a doorway or a window.
Possibly above your computer or cash register to secure information or money.

A *ba-gua mirror* can be placed above your front door to deflect
any bad luck away from your home. If someone enters your home
with ill meaning, those intentions will reflect back at him or her.

Wind chimes and *faceted crystal spheres* disperse ch'i, and sounds
can drive away evil spirits and contrary forces.

Mobiles move stagnant energy about and invoke circulation.
Their use is beneficial to promoting good health.

Hang a mobile in the center of your house if possible, as this is
your health area and can protect the occupants from illness.

The placement of furnishings in a room can determine whether
good luck will bestow a household. Some placements can be altered, while others cannot.

The Bathroom

The location of the bathroom in a house is always a concern in Feng Shui. If located in your wealth corner (the upper lefthand side of your house), your money could be going down the drain! If in the health area (the middle of your home), your health could be negatively affected.

If you can immediately see the toilet when you open your bathroom door, the effect is not good. Hanging a faceted crystal between the doorway and the toilet will diffuse the ch'i that could otherwise encourage health, finances, or romance from going down the toilet!

Also the use of live plants or very realistic artificial plants in the bathroom change the energy of this room as they add life and growth. Decorate your bathroom as best as possible and do not allow it to exhibit a dreary appearance. Keep it bright, clean, and create a happy feeling.

A restaurant owner I know had a failing business and all the advertising he could afford did not seem to bring in more clientele. He hired a Feng Shui expert to furnish some advice. He was told his bathrooms were located in the wealth area of the restaurant.

The bathrooms were always clean and he did not have the room for plants or decorations so he kept the bathrooms very stark. After consulting with the Feng Shui authority, he decided to hire an artist to come in and paint a tropical scene on the walls, as well as on the ceiling. Lots of bright colors and things such as flying birds and tall plants that pointed upward were included. This lifted the ch'i and stopped the flow of energy escaping down the drains. As a result, his business increased and he eventually stopped all advertising, as he could not accommodate all the new customers.

There are several remedies for bathrooms. Keep the doors shut if possible and make sure your bathroom door opens and closes smoothly. People living in a house that has a bathroom door that sticks or gets jammed may suffer from constipation.

Keep the toilet lid down and stoppers in the sinks so symbolically nothing of value escapes into the plumbing. Put small round mirrors over drains or above the toilet as this pulls the energy upward, putting a halt to the good things in your life plummeting down.

Hang a full-length mirror on the outside of the bathroom door, remembering to keep the door closed. If you hang the mirror but keep the door open, you are defeating the purpose. The mirror reflects the ch'i of the rest of the house away from the bathroom so it does not trickle away. It also visually takes the focus away from the bathroom as it reflects a different room.

A Feng Shui practitioner told me there is not really any good location for a bathroom, so almost all bathrooms have to be adjusted to bring up the energy of this space. Use common sense and apply the cure that fits your lifestyle the best.

Kitchen

Another area of concern is the kitchen. And just as mirrors are effective in your bathroom, so it is true in the kitchen. A mirror behind your stove can be most beneficial. The ch'i of your kitchen can also affect your health and your finances, and both need to be guarded from harmful energy.

In her book *Interior Design with Feng Shui*, Feng Shui consultant Sarah Rossbach states that "the logic follows a positive cycle: food feeds a person's health and effectiveness: therefore, the better the food, the more capable the person and the larger his potential income, which will, in turn, improve the quality of his food." She goes on to say, "There can also be a negative cycle: the poorer the person, the worse the food; thus he will earn even less money."

The best placement for a kitchen is in the back of the house, where it is usually calmer and more secure. The best location for the stove is in a position that allows the cook to see anyone who enters the room.

Basically, an island-type stove that a person can stand behind is recommended. However, most of us do not have island stoves so the energy that enters the room hits the stove and the cook from the back or even the side at too strong a pace.

Practically speaking, no one expects you to move your entire kitchen or the stove! So it is here you must apply a remedy if your stove faces a wall.

It is most important that the doorway of your kitchen can be seen when you are at the stove with your back turned. If someone sneaking up from behind startles the chef, it begins a flow of nervous energy that can emanate throughout the household. This nervousness can affect creativity, well-being, income, vocation, and romance. Keeping your back to the doorway as you cook leaves you vulnerable and does not encourage positive vibrations.

In order to provide safety and protection for the person cooking, the best solution is to hang a mirror behind the stove. The mirror should be large enough to reflect all four burners and allow you to see the doorway of your kitchen.

If the stove is not located exactly in a position that will allow you to see the doorway, put a mirror to the side. This also works if your stove does not have room for a mirror behind it. If a mirror of any kind will just not work in your kitchen, hang a wind chime or crystal sphere somehow between the entryway of the kitchen and the stove. This will slow down the ch'i from the kitchen entrance.

Feng Shui experts say there is an added plus to hanging a mirror behind a stove. It can affect the prosperity of the residents in a positive way, as it symbolically doubles the amount of burners; consequently your money should increase.

Even if living alone and cooking little, try to use different burners as opposed to using the most convenient ones. When some of the burners are never turned on, finances may not flourish.

Try to keep your stove as clean as possible and free of obstructions due to stuck food. If your stove is obstructed or blocked, so may your finances be obstructed or blocked!

Bedroom

Your bedroom is a place that also needs to be protected from negative energy or poor ch'i, as this is the place you rebuild your strength.

The position of the bed should be your greatest concern. The bed should lie in a position that gives you the widest view of the bedroom, as well as a view of the door. This encourages a balanced course of ch'i and assures the occupants will not be surprised by anyone entering.

In addition, the placement of your bed in relationship to the door must be considered. In Feng Shui it is advised that your feet do not point straight out the door when you are lying in bed. This is the position in which the Chinese traditionally remove a corpse and can lead to health problems and the demise of a relationship.

If you have no choice and your bed must directly face a door, this can be remedied. Hang a wind chime, crystal, or both in the pathway between the bed and the door. The sound of the chime will divert the onrushing ch'i of the door and the crystal will disperse the energy evenly, creating safety and relief.

Beams over the bed can cause several different types of problems depending on where the beam is located. If it runs down the center of the bed between a couple, it could cause a split in their relationship. If it runs over the head of the occupant, it may cause headaches.

The easiest way to remedy a beam over your bed is to move the bed. If that is not possible, hang bamboo flutes at a 45-degree angle, one on each side of the beam. This lifts the pressure of the beam and promotes better luck and health. The flutes are also knife-like and are said to chase evil spirits away from the occupants, as well as keep them safe from affliction.

Another cure would be to attach red fringe to the entire length of the beam. The color red is active, energetic, and uplifting. This would also negate the unwanted pressure to the body by the oppressive beam.

Every time I think about furniture placement in the bedroom, a delightful real-life story comes to mind. A few years ago a single client of mine not only was having health problems but never seemed to find a lasting relationship. Although she was attractive, intelligent, and had a charming personality, her boyfriends never seemed to last more than a few months and she would soon be "looking" again.

No one could figure out the problem. As she did not live too far from my office, I agreed to go to her house to take a look around. Upon viewing her bedroom, I found what I thought might have been the problem. The foot of her bed was directed straight to the doorway. I also noticed she had only one nightstand, which was on the side of the bed where she slept. I felt this kept the energy of a twosome away from her.

I suggested she should move her bed so it was catercornered to the door and that she add a second nightstand on the other side of the bed.

Six months later I got a call from her. She said moving her bed was the best thing that she had ever done! Her health had improved and she had just gotten engaged. In fact, she met her future husband the day after I visited her home.

"It's amazing how practicing Feng Shui can really make a difference in your life," I said.

"Well, I don't know about that for sure. But in one way or another it worked for me," she said sheepishly.

After asking her to clarify what she was talking about, she explained. She had decided to take my advice and move her bed. Unfortunately or fortunately, she was not strong enough to drag the bed to a different location, so she ventured over to the next-door neighbors' house. They were two very athletic people, and she knew they would be glad to help her.

However, on this particular day, they had a friend visiting them from out of town. It just so happened their friend was single, handsome, strong, and bright! He immediately offered his assistance and escorted her back to her house. Well, the rest is history. He moved not only her bed but also her heart.

There are no guarantees Feng Shui will change your life, but the simplest cures for energy flow are inexpensive and sometimes of no cost at all. Creating the proper flow of energy throughout a living space can shield us from romantic dilemmas, poor career choices, or lack of money and can promote soundness of body and creative endeavors. So why not give it a try? Remember, "If you keep doing what you're doing, you'll keep getting what you're getting!"

Besides the placement of Feng Shui cures, Feng Shui blessings and ceremonies can be utilized as a form of safekeeping and protection for a home or specific location (see "The Orange Peel Blessing Ceremony" in Chapter 10).

PART IV

Diane's Personal Defense Techniques

CHAPTER 14

White Light Protection Techniques

White light is universally symbolic of spirituality, recognition of the truth, and manifestation. It is referred to in all cultures. We hear of "the eternal light," the Savior who is "the light of the world," "I am the light," and "the forces of light and darkness." It is this same light that we must use to protect us from psychic attack. It is white light that will repel, banish, and protect us from negativity.

All techniques of protection using white light are visualization methods. Some people are able to imagine or visualize better than others. As in anything else, the more you practice, the more proficient you will become at imagery.

Standard White Light Technique

This method of defense is what one may call an all-around form of protection that can be used as often as you feel necessary. It is a preventive form of self-defense used when nothing special is going wrong in life and you feel at ease with your environment and the individuals around you. It is like taking supplements to maintain good health. Never take anything for granted.

For this process you do not need anything except a comfortable place to sit. You should be by yourself and the atmosphere should be peaceful and relaxing.

Sit in a chair, sofa, or on the floor, wherever you are most comfortable. Inhale deeply and exhale the air out of your mouth. When you think you have exhaled as much air as possible, push a little harder with one last blow of air. Carry this out three times. As you do this, see any negativity or illness you have being blown out. This rids you of any accumulated psychic sludge you may be carrying.

Now close your eyes and see a white light in the form of a circle or oval covering your entire body. If you would rather stand at this point, do so.

The light should extend at least a foot from your entire being. If you are sitting, remember to imagine it under your chair as well. It must not stop at the physical body but must continue a little farther.

You need not say anything or even think of anything profound. Just see and feel the presence of this protective light. When you sense you have accomplished your goal, get up and continue your day, knowing you are in harmony with all things.

Circle Method

When you are confronted by an influence that is continuously disturbing you, I recommend this banishing method. I am not necessarily speaking of ghosts or even negative influences. Sometimes we are not threatened but are just not at ease. For this purpose, I recommend and distinguish this technique as the circle method.

Perform this approach in the physical space where you feel uncomfortable—if there is a particular spot. If not, perform this ritual anywhere that you feel best. If there is a particular place such as your bedroom and your bed is in the way, do not be concerned. You can draw your circle over anything through the power of visualization. It will settle exactly where it should be.

First you must form a circle that will encompass you. You can be within this area or out of it if you cannot physically fit in the space.

The purpose of the circle formation is that it will not allow anything to drift back into it, as the circle prohibits all from reentering.

Face east as the vibration of the east is the current in which you want to be connected. The vibration from the east is that of new beginnings, building powers, starting over. The sun rises in the east; it replaces the darkness.

Take your second and third fingers together and point at the ground or the floor. With your hand extended like a wand, turn in a clockwise direction and see yourself drawing the circle on the floor as if drawn with a sword that has a blazing glow of white light projected from its point.

Now visualize the circle of light ascending and totally circling the area. It extends out through your roof, through the sky into a universal atmosphere no one can reach. Hold a picture of this circular tube for a few seconds. Then relax and see the circle dissipate. The potency of its light will still remain.

Pyramid of White Light Technique

Pyramids have been revered for their mystical powers. They are made of four triangular faces that meet at a point on the top, usually over a square base.

Interpretations of pyramid power range from studies demonstrating pyramid energy affecting brain rhythms, having healing powers, and having an effect on plants, animals, and water, to extraterrestrial legacies, not to mention associations with the lost continent of Atlantis. Fact or fantasy, most agree the structure has powerful inclinations. Pyramids protect, rejuvenate, and heal. A pyramid of light will accomplish the same thing if your belief is solid.

This approach should be utilized when you are under severe physic attack and feel totally depleted or at a time when your energy is low and you are depressed or down. Remember, this is not an alternative for seeking professional medical or psychological advice. It is something that may be added to any treatment or recommended help you may have been offered.

The pyramid of light is extremely simple. However, from this simplicity emerges great strength and force.

This procedure not only should prevent any more depletion from you mentally, physically, and spiritually, but should replenish you with harmonious and healing vitality.

Take a chair with a straight back and place it in a spacious area. If you have good posture and are flexible, you may opt to sit on the floor with your legs crossed in a lotus or half-lotus position with your spine straight. Whether sitting on the floor or in a chair, keep your shoulders back, face forward, and back straight as possible. Close your eyes and very slowly see a laser-type beam of white light entering the room from above and pointing at the top of your head. Before it touches your head, it starts to expand, encompassing you in the form of a pyramid, running three feet out from all sides. Eventually it is completed, covering you so that you are sitting inside this pyramid of light.

If you have something in particular you are concerned about, now is the time to make your appeal to the universal life force for special protection. For instance: protect me from . . . Repeat your appeal as many times as you feel necessary. When your intuitive self communicates to you that your have been heard, give thanks and rise: your objective has been completed.

CHAPTER 15

Clearing a Space

Earlier in this book I discussed traditional forms of clearing a space and ridding it of negative energy. In this chapter, I will describe another method that I have been using successfully for years.

When deciding to clear a space, I always consider all methods. Since there are several choices, it is best to contemplate the area you wish to clear and than make a decision as to what form of clearing should be used. This is where you must count on your intuition to lead you to the best procedure, ritual, or ceremony. Smudging a space may work on Aunt Jane's house but the method given below may "feel" more appropriate for your own home.

With this method, I clear only on the night of a dark moon or a waning moon. A dark moon is the two or three days when there is no moon in sight at all, just before a crescent moon begins to appear. A waning moon is the phase after a full moon when the moon grows smaller.

As in all the other clearing techniques, the reason you are clearing a space is to dispel negative energy from past owners or a situation of negativity that is persistent. Sometimes it is done as a way to start fresh, even if no unfavorable energy is present. If you are looking to acquire a new job, start a new relationship, or enhance your health, etc., this is an excellent way to prepare for new beginnings.

How to Clear a Space (Diane's Method)

If there is an area outside a building—such as a patio, porch or garden—that you feel also needs to be cleared, use the same procedure. Whether inside a building or outside in the open air, clearing energy is approached the same way. Along with the outside areas, the inside method is identical.

Wear and program one of the gemstones for protection that I recommended in the section on gemstones (Chapter 11). If you do not have the stone in jewelry form, place it in a small pouch with a string around it and hang it from your neck. You could also place it in your pocket or put it in a piece of cloth and safety pin it to yourself.

If you prefer, wear two or more stones. I have worn up to five at a given time based on my intuitive self suggesting I do so. Your intuition gives great recommendations if you listen.

Start from the back of the house or building or the outside perimeters of the area you are going to cleanse. Stand still, close your eyes, and think to yourself, "I clear this space as a copartner with the universal life force."

The reason I recommend you do not say the words out loud is because I have found that the energy you are trying to remove or refresh moves faster when the words are held in your mind.

I have experimented speaking out loud and quietly, and every time the latter works better for me. Try both ways, as we are all unique when it comes to bringing forth our mystical abilities.

Next, imagine a stream of white light descending from the sky covering only your right arm from your fingertips to the very top of your shoulder. This light approaches with a strong and rapid impact. Feel the ability and power your arm has now acquired.

The reason I recommend your right arm is because most of us have been programmed through our lifetime that right is more positive than left. Throughout history the "right" seems to be the superior position. The Bible refers to "the right hand of the Lord," "the right side of the law," and so on and so forth.

I personally am left-handed, but using my right arm for this process is still very comfortable. However, if for physical reasons you cannot use your right arm, the left is fine. If you are just not at ease using your right arm, employ your left. You will not achieve the expected results if you go against your nature.

Add your own ideas that give you a sense of strength and authority. For instance, I usually wrap a piece of black leather around my right arm. As in the Black Candle Ritual, which you will see later in the book (Chapter 19), the color black can be used to dispel and negate. This is my intention in the use of black. I associate leather with longevity, endurance, and protection from the elements. I have associates who are vegetarians or vegan who do not believe in using or wearing leather. This is why options are totally up to you. Fit practices into your lifestyle and your personal belief system.

Select an area in which you would like to begin. Outstretch your right arm, and using big sweeping motions, see yourself moving the negative energy in sheets, out the door or area (if outside). Once you have moved a section, start with the next section. It is comparable to mowing grass.

As you mow, you see where one section has been completed and where you must go next. If you encounter a rounded area or oddly shaped space, use a sweeping action with your arm, like that of a traffic officer directing cars to move along.

Once you feel you have directed this energy away from the area, see it dissipate or disappear. If you do not visualize it vanishing, you may have merely relocated it to a neighbor or building next door. Always, keep other people and places in mind when working with energy. Do not act selfishly.

Afterward, close your eyes and visualize the white light that empowered your right arm leaving rapidly like a rocket upward to a distant location you cannot see. At this time, you may want to say something silently or out loud to complete this rite.

Conclude with something like "new energy to this place, blessings be here," or even a prayer to the God of your understanding. Almost any words of closure would be appropriate. This is the time you should add your distinct touch.

CHAPTER 16

Protecting Others

Healers have been performing long-distance healing for many years. This is the ability to heal a person who is miles away and not in the healer's presence.

We pray with people over the phone for divine intervention to take place in their lives. Reputable psychics have the ability to "do readings" for people who are not sitting with them in person. So it is that we can protect people not present with white light methods of defense.

I had a very interesting experience in connection with protecting others from a distance. You might call it serendipity, a lucky happenstance that turned into this procedure I recommend.

Ten years ago, I knew I was under psychic invasion from an ex-boyfriend with whom I was no longer involved. I could reason he was thinking about me and sending me less than positive thoughts!

I went into my office and sat on a chair in the middle of the room to perform a technique using white light as a protective measure from psychic attack. I formed a circle of salt on the ground around myself and lit a white candle. I visualized the protective light around the circle and all negativity being removed from all that the circle encompassed, which was basically me!

I said, "May my thoughts of defense and healing project themselves out to the universal and may the universal power supply be open to me so negativity is banished and thoughts of this person [I meant my ex-boyfriend] be eliminated." I lit my candle and stared into it for a few minutes until I felt that good was attained.

The next day, however, I still felt this man was burning a hole in my brain. I was quite surprised because usually this technique worked!

I tried numerous times and could not understand the failure. After a week of daily attempts to perfect this procedure, I happened to see a woman I had worked with many years ago at a New Age convention. I commented that she looked wonderful and obviously was in good health on all planes.

She went on to tell me that was not the case at all. She shared the fact that she had been not only very sick but also exhausted and felt as if someone was constantly draining her. "Suddenly one day everything changed," she said joyously. "I don't know what happened or why but I was just a different person overnight!" I interrogated her as to her secret. Was it prayer, rituals, ceremonies . . . what was it? But although she believed in metaphysics, she didn't claim to have done anything unusual.

Having given up on this method of protection, I went back to my pyramid of light procedure I mentioned earlier. This seemed to work for me, but I could not understand where I went wrong.

Having moved only a few weeks previously, I decided to do some deep cleaning now that things were in order. In order to clean the legs of the chair in my office, I turned the chair upside down. There was a photograph stuck to the nails in the bottom the chair. Looking at the photograph, I was amazed to see it was an old picture of the same lady I had just spoken to about her miraculous comeback. Could I have unwillingly helped her? Were my words misunderstood?

The uncanny occurrence that she was suddenly empowered and the fact that her picture was within my circle could have just worked!

From that point I assisted people under psychic assault who were not physically close to me and tried to protect them using a variation of this technique. The reports I received back were more than I had hoped. Hence, I pass this technique to you.

Protecting Others from Psychic Invasion

Once you have determined who it is you want to help, you can discuss it with that individual or you may choose not to advise them of your intent.

There are different thoughts when it comes to asking permission. Many people feel if you are doing something to help someone else and it is for the well-being of that individual, permission is not necessary. Others feel if you are tampering with anyone's aura, force field, or magnetic field, they should be asked.

Another thought is that if someone indicates they need help but have no belief in that which is not visible, it is still appropriate to lend them assistance. The rationale here is that they have indeed implied they do want relief. You must be your own judge. As for myself, I usually ask permission. If they say no, I try to delicately convince them to give it a chance. If no is still the answer, I do not pursue the topic any longer. I recognize it is a path that they must walk as part of their spiritual evolution and I do not interfere.

To carry out this rite, you will need table salt or sea salt, one white candle, and a picture or drawing of the person you are trying to protect. You can use any representation of this individual. I sometimes use a business card or something the person has handled.

Sometimes a gemstone like a clear quartz crystal can be put to use for this purpose. However, it should be cleared and programmed, as discussed in Chapter 11: "Gemstones and Herbs." If there is no representation to remind you of the individual, write his or her name on a piece of paper.

First take a bath or shower, thus cleaning your physical body. Next cover yourself with a white light using the standard method of protection. You must be in harmony and balance to help someone else.

Even if you have analyzed yourself and know you are not totally in balance, you can still proceed. This is providing you do not focus on yourself and for this short time forget about your own needs.

Take your candle, lighter, representation of the intended, and salt to a chosen place in which you will perform this rite.

Place the representation of your intended on the ground behind your candle. In other words, the picture is between you and the candle. Take your salt and in a clockwise direction sprinkle it on the ground, forming a circle. As mentioned before, the circle protects you from negative influences that may flow back at you. Stand or sit in the center of the room. Light your candle.

Say to yourself or out loud: "May my thoughts of defense and healing project themselves out to the universe. May the universal power supply be open to me so negativity is banished from [say the person's name]."

Stare at your white candle for a few seconds and become one with the flame. Feel your energy jutting up as the flame also burns in an upward direction. When you can no longer hold your gaze, say words of conclusion as an end to this ritual. These words should be simple. "And so it is," "Amen," "Blessed be," and "This is truth" are a few examples that may work nicely.

Protective Angel Ritual

If you do not believe in the existence of angels, this is not the method for you. However, I recently read statistics that 80 percent of the planet believe in the authenticity of angels on some level. Therefore, I felt this beloved ritual would be of interest to many readers. This method can be used to protect others as well as yourself.

The things you need for this ritual are only two: love and the faith that you have the ability to call upon help from higher sources when in need. Angels are messengers, protectors, and healers. They are always close-by.

Shower, bathe, or at least wash your hands, face, and feet. You are calling upon the highest of company to come and attend your ceremony.

Sit or stand anywhere you desire: your backyard, your living room, or even your laundry room. Go to a place you want to be. As in previous rites or rituals, there will be a circle that surrounds and protects you. However, this time it will be made up of these celestial spirits.

When you are ready, say nothing. Close your eyes and imagine there are angels suddenly all around you. This should take only seconds. Make it up! Pretend you see them and you really will. How many are there? Try counting them as best you can. This gets you more involved in their essential qualities. It makes you forget about exterior influences and puts the focus directly on them.

If you are intending to help protect someone else, imagine that person or persons in the circle of angels right along with you.

They already know your intention. Therefore, instead of asking for protection, thank them for providing the protection you have been seeking. Bask in the radiant white light that the angels have created. Absorb as much light as you can, as their supply is infinite. Again thank them for their presence and the gift of love and light they shared. See the angels depart, but know they are never far away.

In the spirit of angels, I must include a humorous poem I wrote a few years ago. I was always looking for a sign from the angels to show me they were present. I became quite frustrated because I never received one! Then I realized they need not give signs—I should just "know" they are always with me.

Give Me a Sign

Angels, about front and center.
I need your help . . . I need to center.
Nothing happened. I wasn't loud enough!

Angels, I said again . . . louder than before.
About front and center. I need your help. I need to center!
This isn't working. What don't they get?
What don't I get?

If you're here, give me a sign.
No sign.

Angels, if you're not here, give me a sign.
No sign.

OK Angels, if you *are* here, DON'T give me a sign.
No sign.

I knew they were here!

CHAPTER 17

Power in Numbers and Force Fields

Full Moon Ceremony for Safekeeping and Well-Being

This ceremony can be done as often as you desire on the night of a full moon. This is a preventive way of keeping opposing forces, people, and situations out of your life. I highly recommend this ceremony for two or more people. (If you have a specific concern you need to banish as opposed to this general form of defense, see my Black Candle Ritual in Chapter 19.)

The full moon is the most powerful phase. It is this phase in which we see her entire illuminated face. This is a time of fulfillment, activity, increased psychic ability, celebrations, and projecting our highest intentions. It is a time to put up a force field of positive energy that no one or anything can penetrate. Use the power of the moon to assist you to launch a shield of protection.

Plan in advance. The night of the full moon, everyone involved should have his or her schedule free of other commitments. Know that the reason you are gathering is to protect all those in attendance from potential harm on all levels. One person should be appointed as the group leader or facilitator. This person is responsible for everything being in place and in order. This should be worked out well in advance of the ceremony.

This ceremony is best done outside under the full moon. However, if that is not possible, an inside location will do. If you cannot see the moon from indoors, have a picture or something as a representation of the full moon.

All attending must form a circle. If only two people are participating, face each other. It's okay if some individuals choose to sit in chairs or others opt to sit on the floor or ground. The important thing is that a circle is formed.

You may choose to hold hands. If that is the case, everyone should do so, or no one should hold hands at all. The energy will not be completed if some are holding hands and others are not. Once everyone is in place, the facilitator should take his or her spot inside the configuration and begin the ceremony.

He or she should say:

Close your eyes. As I count up from one to ten, imagine yourself leaving your physical body, and drawing closer to the moon.

One . . . Breathe in deeply . . . exhale slowly.

Two . . . Breathe in deeply . . . exhale slowly.

Three . . . Feel yourself ascending toward the light of the moon.

Four . . . Sense the energy of the moon coming nearer and nearer.

Five . . . Continue to keep your eyes closed, and exhale slowly.

Six . . . As you exhale, imagine any negativity that you now carry, or feel may be projecting toward you in the future, being stopped by a shield of white light.

Seven . . . Feel the vibration of the moon's light. The earth is below. You are very safe . . . a white light encompasses you.

Eight . . . You are now connected with the moon's positive energy. Envision yourself on this luminous sphere. Are you sitting, standing, walking, or merely next to it? Imagine where you are.

Nine . . . Keep your eyes closed. Absorb the power, the life force. You are part of that life force energy, not just an onlooker. You are one with the universe. Take a moment and just be. Try not to think, or imagine anything. [Facilitator should allow about five to ten seconds of silence.]

Ten . . . Continue to keep your eyes closed, and I will now recite our intention. Concentrate.

The facilitator now says:

We are gathered here in this special place to use our cumulative energy to create a force field of white light that will not allow any type of force to penetrate into any area of our lives. It will not perforate our health, work, creativity, finances, or emotional states.

See around our entire group, who have united here tonight, a solid windshield of light that runs in a circle protecting everyone in this circle.

As we depart from this circle, the circle of light will be taken with each and every one of us.

All say together:

And so it is.

The facilitator continues:

Now see yourselves coming back to the earth slowly to the place we started from tonight. (Facilitator must provide a few seconds of silent time.)

Then he or she says:

Once you feel again present, open your eyes and relax.

The facilitator must then ask: "Are we all back?" After everyone has said yes, the facilitator should say, "Now you may leave the circle and relax and reflect on what you just experienced."

If people want to stay in the circle and discuss their experience, they can. This would be an appropriate time to enjoy refreshments and socialize.

The Power of Fours

As a table has four legs, a building has four corners, and a compass has four directions, four is considered a number of stability. This is a rite using four people to create a peaceful environment free from harm's way or to remove unwanted opposing vibrations from a particular person present in the group.

To conduct this rite, you will need three or four people but no less. If you cannot find a fourth party, you can substitute a clear quartz crystal, since it is a conductor of energy and will "hold its own weight," so to speak.

Program it as explained in the section on gemstones. The programming would be with the intention of protection. You cannot use more than one crystal and three people. To attempt to incorporate more crystals and fewer people would not be strong enough to launch this force.

The purpose of this gathering should be to aid one of the four people using strength in numbers or to bring forth an armor of protection for the entire group.

The items you need are a piece of paper, a pen, two envelopes, salt, water, four candles, matches, and if desired, something to extinguish the candles with. The group must all agree as to the reason for their gathering. One person must write it down or type it out on the piece of paper.

It should read like this: "We are gathering here today to bring protection to [say person's name]." If you are not assisting anyone in particular in the group, it should read: "We are gathering here today to bring protection to all of us for [state your purpose]."

Next assign each person a task. There are four tasks. If you have only three people, someone must perform two tasks. They relate to the four astrological elements of the zodiac.

The person's astrological element does not have to coincide with the task. If workable, however, try to match them up the best as possible. Keep in mind the four people performing the rite may all be of the same element! If this is the case, discuss together who feels the most comfortable doing what task and come to an agreement.

> Fire signs: Aries, Leo, and Sagittarius
> Earth signs: Taurus, Virgo, and Capricorn
> Air signs: Gemini, Libra, and Aquarius
> Water signs: Cancer, Scorpio, and Pisces

Task One: The air person must start the music and light the incense.

Task Two: The fire person must place and later light the candles, which are to be placed within the four sides of the square. The first candle should be placed at the midpoint of the top of the square, the second candle midway on the right side, the third midway on the bottom, and the fourth midway on the left side. They should thus form a cross within the square, with each candle corresponding to each of the four cardinal points. Do not light the candles at this stage.

Task Three: The earth person takes the written or typed intention and places it in one of the envelopes and seals it. Then he or she should place it in front of the candle that is positioned at the top of the square.

Task Four: The water person takes a mixture of salt and water and very lightly sprinkles the bases of each of the four candles. Be careful not to wet the wicks.

All participants should stand by and watch the others performing their assignments. No one should leave the room while these responsibilities are being accomplished.

Next each person must stand behind a candle. The air person stands at the top of the square, representing north. The earth person stands to the right of the square, representing east. The fire person stands at the bottom of the square, representing south. The water person stands at the left of the square, representing west.

Once everyone is in place, the air person must cast an etheric or invisible square around the foursome. He or she may use a wand or an athame (a double-bladed knife that has never cut anything solid) or their first and second fingers as a pointer, in the fashion a religious figure would use to perform a blessing.

The caster or person creating the square should start in the east, where everything begins, using the chosen pointer and draw his or her invisible square around the group and everything that will remain in the square, eventually ending where he or she started. It is important that the candles are always included on the inside of the square and are set at the north, south, east and west in a cross formation.

Next, the air person lights his or her candle with a match or lighter. Then the air person lights the earth person's candle with the candle that has just been lit. The earth person lights the fire person's candle, and the fire person lights the water person's candle. The candles should be set back on the floor. Everyone should be then be seated in their chairs or on the floor. Each person should sit behind the candle but still within the square. At this time, all may join hands if the group has chosen.

The actual rite is as follows:

1. The air person says out loud: "Protect us." Then the earth person says out loud: "Protect us." The fire and water people follow suit.

2. The air person says out loud: "We banish all negative forces," the earth person repeats "We banish all negative forces," and the rest follow.

3. The air person says out loud: "We shield ourselves in light." The earth, fire, and water people follow suit.

4. (If there is one person in particular you were assisting in psychic protection, recite these words. If not, skip this step.) The air person says out loud: "We protect [say person's name] through our unity. We are one with her or him." The rest individually repeat these words as before.

5. The air person should ask the group to visualize a white light in the form of a square completely encompassing the four attendants. He or she then says out loud: "We are safe, we are restored, we are a union of light." Each individual repeats the words out loud in the usual order.

6. Lastly, the air person says out loud: "Nothing can penetrate the light." Each repeats as before.

Everyone now can discontinue holding hands. The air person rips the envelope one time in half and hands it to the earth person. The earth person rips it again and hands the pieces to the fire person. The fire person rips it and hands it to the water person. The water person rips it and hands it back to the air person. The air person places the pieces in the unused envelope. In order, starting with air, each person extinguishes his or her candle. Use something to snuff it out (which you should already have in place next to you) or put your finger in front of the flame and blow so the wax will not scatter. The air extinguishes the flame from the sides.

Now the group has two choices, but should decide this well before the rite. They can burn the envelope inside or outside in a fireproof container, or submerge the envelope in water and dispose of it as they wish.

Once the envelope has been sent out into the cosmos, all must go back to where they were standing or sitting in front of their extinguished candle, join hands, and one by one, starting with air in the regular order, say: "We are cocreators with the universe."

At this point, all should feel an unusual type of energy, which will within seconds turn into a feeling of safety and confidence that anything can be accomplished.

CHAPTER 18

Throwing Energy

Throwing energy is an excellent form of defense against a variety of misfortunes that may come your way. It is uncomplicated and direct. You can perform this action anywhere and anytime with the throw of your hand.

Energy emanates from your hands, and when you learn to apply it with intention, you can push arrows of aggression away from yourself, another person, or a situation.

Reiki masters have been using the energy from their hands for years as a form of wholistic healing. Reiki means "Universal Life Energy." It is the transforming of a person's entire essence.

What I am suggesting is not Reiki but a method that has a similar belief: that the use of our hands as a conduit of energy is a very worthy endeavor.

To "throw energy," you must be determined and strong of mind. Anyone in a state of weakness, be it from illness, depression, or suffering from high anxiety, may have a difficult time with this mode of psychic response.

Throwing energy is the philosophy that you can stop negative energy coming toward you before it reaches your physical body or anything or anyone in your view that you are trying to protect.

It is like looking at the street from a high-rise building. You see a person on foot ready to turn around a corner while someone else on a bicycle is going to turn at the same time. You feel there is nothing you can do to stop these two people from colliding. All you can do is watch, as there is no time to run down and warn anyone.

When you throw energy, you cannot visibly see it. However, if you could, it would appear as if you were spraying a water hose at a fire. The water reaches the flames before they are able to come too close to you. The situation or person is the flame and you are the water.

We have all had this same experience in years of driving. Imagine yourself approaching a busy intersection. You have just gotten the green light. You proceed to cross the intersection but you have a "feeling" someone from either direction is not going to stop. You feel somewhat helpless but proceed cautiously. This is where throwing energy can be very beneficial. When driving, I use this method repeatedly.

If you are approaching a turn, intersection, hill, or driving situation you are very uncomfortable in, first logically use all caution

Throwing Energy While Driving

and execute your basic driving skills. Then, throw energy to both sides of the street. To do this, keep both hands on the steering wheel. Keep your thumbs and palms on the wheel and quickly lift your fingers out and away. Sense the energy propelling out with lightning speed to stop anything that may be intending to come your way. This can also be done if riding in someone else's vehicle. Just wave one or both hands in a backstroke of sorts. Some may say the motion is similar to shooing flies away!

Another time to throw energy is when you witness a situation involving other people. The lady crossing the street is not paying attention to the red light and starts to walk toward the traffic, lost in thought. You are too far away to yell beyond the traffic or to catch her in time. Throw energy toward her to stop her from continuing her approach.

This takes some practice and may sound too easy to conceive. It is not easy and does require practice on a regular basis. It is difficult to explain an exact method other than visualizing white light flowing out of your hands in a brisk manner. The reason is, there is a unique feeling that you must find from within. When you know what you must sense in order to make this work, you will tap into that same power each time and eventually master this method.

At the risk of sounding romantic, it is comparable to meeting someone for the first time and knowing you may be falling in love or lust. Something starts to stir inside you that triggers an energetic current.

You remember the last time you had that feeling you got married in six months! However, your friend might have a similar encounter but have no interest at all. Energy works differently in all of us.

So is the nature of throwing energy. What I recommend may be perfect for me but you will not feel that same link. This is why you must practice this method daily. You will begin to remember what works for you. Such as the time you waved your hand and saw the light rush out of it and a truck came to a sudden halt. You will build confidence as you see more and more successes.

Not to stray too far from the subject of psychic protection, but here is a story about how this throw of force can quiet noises in nature and accomplish more than one may ever realize.

A friend and I once attended a serious business meeting, which for some reason was held outdoors. Unfortunately, the sounds of birds, frogs, and crickets were very loud and distracting. The speaker could hardly be heard and the organizers were starting to scurry about to see if the building on the property was available for us to relocate. Meanwhile, the noises got louder and louder.

While everyone else was fretting, my friend and I threw up our hands when no one was looking and threw energy out to the perimeters. The noises stopped completely. Later that evening a gentleman came up to the two of us and asked us what we had done. "Done about what?" I questioned. He said, "I saw you girls wave your hands and the noise stopped immediately!" We said we must have been stretching, but he didn't believe it.

CHAPTER 19

Black Candle Ritual to Dispel Negativity

Light a black candle. It burns down slowly and mysteriously. It somehow commands respect. As the black candle burns and gradually diminishes, so can the negative aspects in your life. Does it sound too easy to believe? Does it suggest something evil or Satanic? Well, it shouldn't.

The thought of burning a black candle can make some people shiver. Why aren't black candles used more often? Yes, there are those who have an understanding of them, but most of us know little about the true positive uses they offer. It is not Satanic ritual. It is not about death or evil. It is a means to an end, the end of negativity.

So let's give the very misunderstood black candle a bit more credit. Let's take it out of the closet, put it on the table, and light it up. It is one of the mystic's best-kept secrets and the beginning of enabling a psychic shield of protection.

I have found the black candle best for dispelling negative vibrations that have attached themselves to your being through no particular person, but rather from an object, place, or piece of clothing. If you are sensitive and leave yourself unprotected, every time you accidentally brush against someone, you may be picking up his or her vibration from their coat sleeve. Certain structures can give off a vibration that can permeate your aura. Certain objects that have been handled by someone else can still hold their energy, which you may absorb like a sponge.

After a while, all these little bits of psychic debris will start to accumulate and you will find yourself feeling the only luck you have is bad luck!

There can be such a covering of old accumulated litter that any positive advantage will be unable to filter through. You have heard people say they feel they always have a "black cloud" hanging over their heads. Well, maybe it is not literally a black cloud but they can feel the heaviness of a negative magnetic force encompassing them.

To merely advise someone to take a positive attitude and think happy thoughts is fine in theory, but the subconscious needs more than that. This is why I suggest a ritual using an object that will, for a positive outcome, represent the negative conditions in your life. This ritual is not a means of removing people from your life (I address that later in the book), but a means of cleansing what, to coin a phrase, some would describe as "bad luck."

By performing this method of clearing the atmosphere, you are also setting up a clean space to protect yourself from a recurrence. This process is intended to disengage all the baggage and opposing paraphernalia of the psyche that has hampered your trek through life.

This method should be done on the night of a full moon, dark moon (two or three days before a new moon when the moon is not visible at all), or when the moon is waning (diminishing in size from full to a crescent moon).

The moon's vibrations will act as a springboard to aid you in your endeavor. I recommend performing this ritual monthly as preventive maintenance or at the very least when you start feeling yourself getting off balance.

Black Candle Ritual

Note: Read this entire section before conducting this ritual.

Getting Started—Things You Will Need

- One black candle that can stand alone or be used in a holder. Self-made or store-bought.

- Matches or a lighter.

- A candle snuffer or a cup to snuff out the candle.

- A chair if you do not want to sit on the floor. Crossing the legs is optional, as this is not meditation.

- Music and incense (optional).

What Type of Black Candle to Use

Any style will do. Just make sure the candle has the ability to stand by itself with or without a candleholder. I find a small votive or dinner candle is the best for me.

These days you can purchase black candles much more readily than in the past. I have even seen them at candy stores (licorice scented). Shop around. The cost is nominal, and unscented or scented does not matter.

If you are really ambitious and have the time, you may want to make your own black candles. There is nothing better than putting your own personal energy into a project from start to finish. This is why I felt it was important to provide a means to create your own black candles. However, I did seek out professional advice!

After talking to several candle makers, I was fortunate to come in contact with an expert living in Scotland named Kenneth Clark. His energy and meaning were so positive you could feel the strength and balance through his candles.

After explaining my intention, Kenneth was kind enough to provide me with two methods of making black candles. He mailed me the directions for these candles from the Sanquhar Post Office in Scotland, the world's oldest post office, established in 1738. This is where his candlery is located. Upon receiving them, I could feel the vibration of days gone by on the very paper.

The directions carried with them a lively energy, just what is needed to negate the things in life we don't want. I feel his techniques are more than just directions on how to make a candle. I feel he passes on this vitality to all those who use his guidance!

Kenneth Clark's Method for Making a Black Pillar Candle

Things You'll Need

- Newspapers.
- Paraffin wax (you can get this from a craft or hobby shop).
- Black candle wax dye block (you can also get this from your craft or hobby shop).
- An old jug for pouring
- Wick.
- Scissors.
- A *small* aluminum pillar mold (you can buy these at a craft or hobby shop; make sure if you are buying an aluminum pillar mold that you get a base stand with it).
- An old pot.
- An old large tin can (coffee can, etc.).
- Plasticine/play putty clay (kids' clay).
- A lollipop stick.
- Oil-based perfume, if desired. Although the candle is being burned to dispel negativity, if you enjoy a special fragrance or aroma . . . include it. This is all about making you feel better.

Method

- Cover the table you will be working on with newspaper to keep it protected.
- Cut the wick to a larger length than the pillar mold.
- Assemble your mold to its base.
- If your wax is in a block form, break it up with a hammer so it can fit into your tin can.

- Put your old pot on the stove and fill the bottom approximately a quarter full of water.

- Put your tin can into the water (creating a double boiler) and put some of the wax blocks into it. Do not fill the tin can full of the wax chunks. It may overflow as it melts!

- *Very slowly* bring the water to a boil, making sure that your pot doesn't run out of water. You are basically melting the wax as you would melt chocolate in a double boiler.

- Once you can see the wax melting, add more chunks so you have enough wax to fill your mold. *As you add your additional chips of wax, think about the reason you will burn this candle in the future. What is the intention? What are you trying to dispel? Visualize yourself putting that intention into the pot.*

- Once you feel you have enough wax melted, turn off the heat and dip your wick into the melted wax, making sure it's soaked through. Take care not to burn yourself.

- Hold the wax-coated wick by one end, allowing it to hang vertically. Hold it for a few minutes to allow the wick to harden and become stiff.

- Once the wick is firm, thread it through the hole in the top of your pillar mold, allowing about an inch sticking out the top. Seal the gap of the top of your mold using your play putty. *As you seal the gap, think that you are sealing all the things about this situation that you do not want to return or be continued.*
  (Remember the mold will be upside down. The top will be the bottom, and the bottom will be the top, as all pillar molds rest upside down in their base holders.)

- Put some of your black wax dye into the molten wax and stir with an old metal spoon. Keep adding the dye until you get the desired strength of color. (You can also add perfume or aroma at this stage if desired.)

- Using an oven glove, carefully lift the can out of the pot and pour the wax into your old jug.

- Pour the wax from your old jug into the metal pillar mold, holding the wick central at all times.

- Place the lollipop stick over the top of the mold and let the wick lie over it, making sure the wick is in the center of the pillar.

- Make sure you have some wax left over. As wax starts to set, it will create a crater, which you may wish to fill up, and it's best to do this throughout the setting time. If left till the wax has completely set, it tends to crack the whole candle. It's also wise to keep checking that your wick is tight and central at all times.

- When the wax is set and the mold completely cool, turn it over and remove the sealing putty, squeeze the mold, and the candle should fall out.

- Remove the lollipop stick and cut the wick at the base of your candle. Trim the wick at the top to approximately 5 millimeters.

- Make sure your old pan is completely dry, and put it on a low heat. Then firmly press the base of your candle into the pot, melting the bottom of the candle so it will stand up straight. This can be quite tricky to do, but do not be too concerned as this candle is not for decorative purposes.

- Once you're happy that your candle will stand straight, set it aside for the day you choose to do your Black Candle Ritual.

Note:

- Wax is a very flammable substance.

- Never use water to extinguish a wax or oil fire.

- Always ask your craft or hobby shop assistants for correct thickness of wick for thickness of candle.

Kenneth Clark's Method for Making a Black Oil-Burning Candle

In this method we color the *water* black as opposed to the candle! No wax is necessary and therefore there is little cleanup. The candle burns on the black water and oil, dispelling negativity in a somewhat different manner. However, the intention is just as strong.

For those who do not want to deal with wax, this is a fun and powerful method Kenneth recommends. I really enjoy this one.

Things You'll Need

- Newspapers.

- A tall jar, such as a spaghetti jar (make sure the glass is thick so it will withstand hot water; thin glass may break).

- Aluminum foil.

- Cooking oil, such as sunflower.

- Wick.

- Water-based poster paint.

Method

- Cover the table on which you will be making the candle with newspaper to protect it.

- Using your scissors, cut a circle from the aluminum foil a size smaller in diameter than the tall jar you will be using. Once cut out, turn up the edge of the foil circle to make a lily pad–type shape. This will allow it to float. Put a small hole in the center of your foil lily pad.

- Cut your wick about an inch long and thread it through the hole in your foil lily pad. Leave only about 5 millimeters of wick sticking out the top of your foil lily pad.

- Boil a kettle or pot of water for a few minutes then allow it to cool down a bit.

- Slowly fill the tall jar to within an inch of the top.

- Put some of your black water-based paint in the water and stir until the water turns black. *This black water will represent the negativity you are attempting to retract. It will dissipate as the floating candle burns.*

- Pour your cooking oil into the water, allowing the tall jar to fill almost to the top; it should look as if you have put in about half an inch of oil from a side view.

- Float your silver foil lily pad in the center of the tall jar and leave it for a few minutes, allowing the wick to soak up the oil.

- Once the oil has found its way to the top of your foil lily pad, you should be able to light it and use it for your Black Candle Ritual.

I do understand that most of you reading this book are not looking to be professional candle makers. Nevertheless, if you feel like tapping into that creative side of yourself, give it try. I have tried these processes several times and have had great success. My candles may not come out looking beautiful but I must tell you I feel they are very powerful. Remember you are not looking for elegance but for meaning.

Note: If your candle is not straight, not balanced, and not beautiful, I could not think of a more perfect representation for the very elements you are trying to eliminate from your life. You have made a perfect candle for you. There are no mistakes!

Black Candle Ritual

- Purchase or make your black candle.

- Choose a day when you will have at least forty-five minutes to an hour of private and quiet time. Remember the phase of the moon is most important. Perform this ritual day or night when the moon is waning . . . decreasing from a full moon to a new moon or the night of a dark moon, when there is no visible sign of the moon at all.

- Cleanse yourself. Take a shower or a bath, if possible. If this is not possible, at least wash your hands, face, and feet. What you're doing is not just bathing but creating a *rite*, since your intention is not merely to cleanse your physical body but to go beyond the physical plane and cleanse that which is around you. As you wash or shower, visualize all the sorrow and negativity in your life being taken out of your body and mixing with the water. Then see it passing down the drain.

- If bathing, think of the negative energy you have absorbed loosening on your body. Then, take a shower after you bathe to assure it is removed. If in a natural body of water (lake, ocean, river, stream, etc.), see the negetive energy dispersing into the larger body, where it will immediately become insignificant in comparison to what is around it, which diminishes it.

- Dress comfortably in clean cotton or a garment made of natural fabric, as these are of nature. If these fabrics are not available, wear a favorite item of clothing that is clean and you "just like." If secluded, you can be nude if you're comfortable.

- Shut your phones off and select a serene place inside. This ritual can be done outside, but unless it is an almost windless night, I would not suggest it.

- If you are uplifted by music and certain melodies enable you to relax and get into an altered state of consciousness, play some mediation, New Age, chanting, or classical music. You may want to light incense. I recommend honeysuckle as it aids in the releasing action. Start your music now and light your incense.

- Put a chair in the middle of the floor where you intend to conduct this ritual or you can choose to sit on the floor. Whether you cross your legs or not is of no importance as this is not meditation.

- Place your candle, matches, lighter or floating candle on a solid table or area so as not to tip. If sitting on the floor, set everything down near the spot where you will be sitting.

- Face north, as it is the most powerful direction of the compass. Before lighting the candle, use it as a wand by holding the bottom with your left hand so the wick points away from you. This can be done whether in a container or not.

- If you are using a floating candle or oil candle, use the second and third fingers of your right hand to form your wand.

- Pointing to the ground with your wand, turn *counterclockwise* (beginning at twelve o'clock and turning to eleven, ten, etc.) and draw an imaginary circle on the floor with you inside it. This circle should encompass you and the chair or a space large enough in which you can sit.

Note: The reason I say counterclockwise, which is very seldom used in any ceremonies (and some may not agree with), is because you are taking the negativity away from your future. You do not want it to move through time with you. This is of the utmost importance.

- Once you have formed your mystical circle, sit in your chair or on the floor and light your candle. It should be directly in front of you. It can be on the ground or on a table. Whatever works for you. The music and the incense need not be in the circle. *Do not step out of your circle.*

Note: The next part of this ceremony is what I like to think of as non-denominational. It is intention with a spiritual approach. Whether you follow an organized religion or choose to consider yourself a "spiritual person" but not religious is of no importance. The belief in a higher power of some nature is all that is necessary.

- Light your candle and say out loud or to yourself: "In the Name and with the Power of [fill in who or what you consider your higher power], remove all negativity that surrounds me. I believe this true."
- Envision very quickly a surge of crystal light flowing from your toes to your waist to your shoulders and out and over the top of your head. This should take only seconds.
  For this technique I do not think it necessary to go through a series of deep breaths and a slow ascent of energy. I believe it needs to go quickly and precisely.

I feel some individuals do not give their minds enough credit. We can get to an altered state quickly with the right intention. Slowly and tediously is not my philosophy. It leaves people frustrated and bored. (This is not meditation. It is releasing negativity and replacing it with positiveness.) Meditation is when we listen . . . and we are not listening at this time . . . we are doing and releasing!

- As the white light rushes through our essence, it simultaneously is pushing the negative vibrations out. Right out the top of your head. See it as a volcano of black tar erupting out the very peak of your head. When you feel it is all gone and only white light starts to flow, visualize an angel, the God of your understanding, the god/goddess, or the universal life force placing a crystal hand on your head and sealing the white light within you.

- If you do this, you have achieved much for one day. If the first time it does not work or you don't feel you have made progress, be relentless in your efforts and try again at another time.

- Now just sit for as long as you feel is necessary and stare at your candle or close your eyes and feel the positive energy. You should start to feel empowered and hopeful.

- When leaving your space, if your candle has not burned out by itself, snuff it out with your cup or candle snuffer. Or if necessary, you can extinguish it by putting your finger in front of the flame and then blowing. This way the air goes around your finger, hitting the flame from the sides, and does not cause a push of air. Since your breath and the flame are both creative energies, it can be too much creative force going in one direction and can pierce your circle.

- Stand up and remove your circle. Extend your arms straight out in front of you about 24 inches apart, with your palms up, and make a lifting motion as far as you feel comfortable. Visualize the circle coming up from around your feet and being launched into space, where it will dissipate. Remember your circle is always for good intention (or should be!) so you are not sending anything into the ether that is not of a positive nature.

- Burn the candle until your intuition tells you it has done its job. If you have any part of your candle left, *do not save it. Do not bury it.* Drench what is left in water and put it in a plastic bag you can tie or wrap it in aluminum foil. Then, remove it from your house as soon as possible, even if it is just outside the door or window until the next day or whenever your trash is removed.

If using an oil candle, disassemble it and dispose of it the best way you see fit.

If you have chosen to make your own candle, to dispose of the remaining part may seem like a lot of hard work for a ritual that does not last too long! You must keep in mind, though, that the negativity to your situation took much longer than the time it took to form your candle! The results will be well worth the effort.

Note: If your candle should burn out before you have completed the ritual, merely relight it. You do not have to say anything or start over. It will hold its potency until you are finished.

Special Note: If You Are Interrupted

If something happens or the doorbell rings and you cannot ignore it, put out your candle and, using your right hand, quickly point your second and third fingers at any point on the circle and draw an imaginary door or gate that will open the circle, allowing you to leave. Walk through your etheric door and tend to what you need to do. Come back to your circle if time permits, entering the same way you left. With the same fingers close your circle, relight your candle, and continue. Your circle will hold your intention until you return (but not over 15 minutes). If you cannot continue, take your right hand, palm down, and pass it over the entire circle, moving it in a slight upward motion as if tracing the letter J (this passes the partial energy you had started to create back into the life force to neutralize itself). The next time you must start over from the beginning. This is not a problem; it is merely going back to the starting line.

CHAPTER 20

Name Utilization Ceremonies: Blessings and Christenings

The moment you give a boat, car, airplane, home, commercial establishment, or even a computer a name, you give it life. Anything you attach a name to will start to respond to your mood swings as you have bestowed upon it an energy of its own. This includes living things. Maybe you heard this before: "Don't give that stray cat a name, or you'll be stuck with it."

When we name something we have feelings for, it is our nature to take care of it, as well as to protect it. Treat it with respect and dignity. The best way to do this is to name it properly from the beginning. Anything can be christened or blessed.

I consider myself spiritual with a belief in God, but I do not follow any one organized religion. I think all religions that teach you not to harm anyone willingly and encourage you to love your fellow man or woman are good beliefs.

It is all the same higher power; we just take different roads to make our way home.

Sai Baba said it beautifully,

There is only one religion: The Religion of Love.
There is only one caste: The Human Race.
There is only one language: The Language of the Heart.
There is only on God: He is Everywhere.

As I believe there is only one God or higher power, I also believe we can cocreate with our God. Hence, we have the ability to perform our own blessings and christenings as well as employing those of valued religious figures.

If you are a member of a religious or spiritual group, you may want to ask a holy leader that you respect to bless or christen something. Their intentions are true and they certainly are professionals in this area. However, if you name everything that walks through your door, calling upon your favorite pious figure might get to be a bit overwhelming for him or her.

I feel anything given a name should have a spiritual ceremony attached to it. This enlivens the energy of the person, pet, or object.

Different people are gifted in different areas. Their energy is more conducive in some fields as opposed to others.

If you decide not to do your own christening, blessing, or clearing, make sure the individual you include is of true intention and wishes the best for you and whatever it is you are having named.

When you have in your possession something new or preowned, you must clear it of any past energies that it may have absorbed. If it is preowned, the energy of the past owner and all those who came in contact with it will still linger.

If it is new, the numerous people who had been connected with it may have involuntarily deposited their energy upon it. That being said, if that energy is not of a positive nature, the strength of whatever you have named won't be positive either.

When my fiancé, Adrian, and I moved into our new house, we blessed it by way of many faiths. We used holy water his mother had given him from a Catholic church in Barbados. We smudged it with white sage in Native American style and waited for a new moon to perform this ceremony. I planted crystal quartz in the ground to promote positive energy, and we finally utilized Feng Shui to promote "good ch'i." We have never been so happy in such a tranquil and blessed location.

If your intention is pure, you can create your own ceremony or ritual to bless or christen a place or living thing. Nevertheless, I have included a few ceremonies that I have been practicing for years. Many individuals who practice these same ceremonies have found great satisfaction.

Remember, even if you do not choose to name something, you can still bless and protect it.

As I write this book, it appears that real-life experiences keep generating that I cannot help but include. I prefer to write of my own experiences, as well as those of others, since then not everything is secondhand information.

After the section you read now was completed, a situation arose that compelled me to come back and include it in this chapter. "Practice what you preach" is the expression that fits the following report I now present. I very honestly will tell you I made a mistake. I did not heed my own advice. It could have caused me and my fiancé disaster at sea! Here's my story:

Adrian and I were fortunate enough to find a small boat that we had been longing for. It was preowned but was within our modest budget and exactly what we had hoped to find. Adrian is a marine surveyor with over twenty years' experience surveying boats and being around the water. He managed a marina in Granada some years back and was not new to boating.

I love the water as it soothes my soul and lifts my spirit. We drove past a small marina and there it was . . . the perfect boat. The for-sale sign beckoned us from the street. We pulled into a parking area next to the marine store and examined the vessel. The store was closed so we wrote down the telephone number, to call later.

I knew from that moment that this boat was to be ours. We were both a bit apprehensive, assuming the boat would be over our budget. However, as I believe anything is possible, we made the call.

The boat was definitely older but the engine had been recently rebuilt. It did not have a name but this is not unusual. Not all owners name their boats.

We made an offer on the vessel and were waiting for an answer. While our offer was pending, we went out to the boat and I put my energy all around it. The boat was on a trailer, not in the water. With palms flat down on the bow, I projected my intention to purchase the boat on to the vessel. I followed suit on the aft, starboard, and port sides. I saw us on the boat, taking care of the boat and being happy.

We came to an agreement with the owner and purchased the craft. Naturally, I wanted to perform a boat blessing. I would remove all old energies from previous owners and then bless the boat in the method given below. However, we needed to get the boat home.

I normally would have recommended blessing the boat first to anyone, before setting out to sea. Or at least temporarily protecting it with white light before leaving the dock. However, our house was less than ten minutes away from the marina and I opted to wait until the boat was at our dock.

The day we picked up the boat was cloudy and dismal. I was so excited about our new purchase I brought no forms of protection. I never even thought to protect the boat with the simplest "white light" technique, as my excitement overshadowed my normal thought process.

We left the marina and the engine was running well. Instead of going directly home, we decided to anchor for a while to enjoy the water and our new boat and to investigate its functions. The skies were gray but the waters were calm. Neither lightning nor thunder was present, so we chose not to rush home. It was there that we decided to name the boat "White Light" in honor of my first book, the same book you hold in your hands. What a great name for a boat. With a name like that, the boat could not help but be protected!

As we sat proudly in our new vessel, it came to me that we had bought the boat, taken it from previous owners who had had it in their family for years, and no one had ever told the boat what was transpiring. This may sound foolish to some, but I mean to speak in silence and energetically, not verbally.

I let the thought that we had not asked permission pass for the moment, because I knew we were minutes from home. I would carry out the boat blessing later that day and ask the boat permission to name her "White Light."

Suddenly a bolt of lightning filled the sky. I was touching metal and got a slight shock to my arm! Adrian commented, "God must be trying to give us a message about something!" Although he spoke those words in jest, I realized it was a serious and clear message. We had never blessed the boat! I had put my energy into the boat so as to be able to purchase it, but we never did a thing to safeguard the vessel.

We never asked permission—no prayers, no ritual, no ceremony, and not even a temporary light encompassing this longed-for vessel!

Out from nowhere the sky grew almost black. The clouds above us were a strange chestnut brown in color and appeared weightless yet strong. The clouds seemed to be moving very cautiously in large sheets.

We decided to make our way home. The boat was running well and we quickly passed the mile markers that were leading us to our destination. A bit of lightning started to appear and the sound of thunder filled the skies. This concerned us but we were so close to home it did not cause great alarm or worry.

Suddenly with a crash of thunder and a flash of lightning, the motor just stopped! "Adrian," I called, "why did you turn off the engine?"

"I didn't," he replied. "It just froze."

I said in a lighthearted tone, "This is a lot of fun for our first time out to sea with the boat."

Adrian said in a serious voice, "Look at those clouds. They could turn into water spouts." Then the clouds started to funnel as if a tornado was forming and there we sat numb in the water. We dropped anchor so we wouldn't drift while Adrian tried to start the engine, but to no avail. I went and sat down, and after taking three deep breaths, I visualized a white light encircling the boat. I imagined huge shields of white light pushing against the clouds, as if driving them back. I was totally focused on my goal in a complete state of altered consciousness.

When I finally opened my eyes, I looked down at the water. Out of nowhere emerged four dolphins. They sprang forward from the gray waters as guides or protectors. At that point all fear left me and I felt at peace. Using a cellular phone, we called for help and someone from the marina was soon on their way to tow us into port.

Nevertheless, we knew that it would be a little while before they would arrive. The clouds began to swirl and we were right in the path of what could be a potential twister.

The temperature started to drop and the winds were picking up. The dolphins seemed to stay with us and I wondered if I could telepathically communicate with these amazing creatures.

Perhaps they knew how these scrolling clouds were going to behave. I once again sat in an altered state and visualized a laser of light beaming to one of the dolphins right between its eyes.

I chose not to tell Adrian what I was doing because it did not seem to be the time to discuss telepathic communication with dolphins! Somehow I did not think he would appreciate the opportunity I found in this situation.

I continued to throw my beam of light and silently asked, "Are these clouds going to turn into a giant water spout?" I waited but nothing happened. Then I suddenly felt an answer. "Things will be fine."

Was I making this up in my mind, because this is what I wanted to hear? I sensed a male voice and heard it again. Maybe I was just "losing it" and needed to give my constant need to experiment with the unknown a break!

All of a sudden we could see the rescue boat coming toward us. When the two gentlemen from the marina got to the boat, I tried again to make light of the situation. "I know there is higher purpose in this situation, but I don't know what it is yet."

Virtually ignoring me, all they could do was look at the clouds. "Doesn't look good," one commented, as his face paled.

In a rush they secured our boat to theirs. It now started to rain. The dolphins were gone but I knew everything was fine. I very calmly just sat down and enjoyed the ride back. We arrived at the boatyard in safety and were driven home.

That evening I spoke to Adrian of how we did not bless our boat before we set off for our excursion. However, nothing could now be done, with the boat at the marina.

We were now concerned about the state of the motor, as this could be a costly expense. That night I could not sleep. It seemed to be too late to save the boat from major repairs.

I closed my eyes and astrally projected myself to the boat. I asked the boat for permission to own her and name her. I got a yes. I saw myself walking through the boat clearing energy away and performing a boat blessing and christening. I brought myself back to the bed in which my physical body lay and went to sleep.

It was a weekend so we had to wait until Monday to get the diagnosis about the engine from the mechanic. As I sat at my computer writing this very section, the telephone rang. It was the marina. They said the engine had some problems but they would basically rebuild the engine at no expense to us. This was above and beyond the duty of the marina as they were not responsible for this used boat. In fact, the owner was selling it for a friend and not as a part of his actual marine business.

Such kindness overwhelmed us. This meant the boat was a better value than we had ever anticipated. It was like giving the vessel a heart transplant. It would be healthier than ever. The boat surely wanted us to own her. The boat will be returned to us in two weeks. Before we start that motor, we will perform the christening below.

Blessing and Christening Ceremony for a Boat (or Any Mode of Transportation)

If you are blessing a plane, a car, or another form of transportation, the ceremony is the same. Just substitute where you need to.

Naming a new boat or naming a boat that never had a name is one thing. However, you may have heard that renaming a boat is bad luck or so say some very superstitious sailors and boaters. This is one reason we conduct boat blessings.

Since the Queen of England will most likely not be available to christen your boat, you may want to look for other sources or do it yourself. This is one of my most enjoyable ceremonies.

Whether it is day or night is not important. However, if you can adjust your schedule around a full, waxing, or new moon, it is all the better. These phases promote power, strength, and new beginnings.

First you must clear the vessel of any trace of the previous owner's energy, if a used craft. If new, you must still clear the boat of any trace of energy from the other people who may have worked on the boat or boarded her for any reason after your new ownership.

Some ceremonies feel old boat log books or anything with the old owner's name should be removed. This is a splendid idea but sometimes not practical. So by clearing it in the following fashion, you will neutralize those energies and they will be null and void.

Note: If renaming a boat, the old name should be removed completely and the new name placed on her before this rite. This blessing will enliven the boat.

Things You Will Need

Flowers or Flower Petals: Any kind, providing they are real.

A balloon: Use if denaming her (removing her old name). Fill it with helium so it will float into the air when released. I have seen people purchase butterfly balloons, bird-shaped balloons, and all different shapes. However, a regular round balloon from a package works too. The bigger the boat, the bigger the balloon. You may want to have a backup in case your balloon pops. But you will use only one balloon—no bunches.

Champagne: Work within your budget but try to use real champagne, not sparkling wine. You will not be drinking any part of this, so if you want a toast later, I would advise getting an extra bottle for yourself and guests.

Note: I must again reiterate the importance of doing some form of protection before leaving the place where you made the purchase. You can wait until a special date or wait until you go to that special location before performing this christening. However, at the least, protect the boat with a white light as a temporary measure before the formal ceremony.

Attendants: You can have as many people there as you wish or do this quietly by yourself. If performing parts of this ceremony by yourself leaves you uncomfortable due to people in the area, make changes. This is not written in stone and there is no right or wrong way. The speaking of the words is the most important thing.

Music: If you choose to play music, it must be something calm such as classical, New Age, Celtic, meditation, or whatever you like that is instrumental or has just a bit of singing or chanting included. Test your musical system before the ceremony to make sure it is working. Do not use a radio as it may break into a commercial.

Some go as far as to have a live musician perform. Use your sources. Most people find recorded music works just beautifully.

Be peaceful and respectful of this ceremony. The merriment can come afterward.

Boat Blessing and Christening Ritual

Step One: Clear the Vessel from Previous Energies.

Use the smudging ritual in Chapter 10: "Rituals and Ceremonies," or use my personal method in Chapter 15: "Clearing a Space."

Step Two: Release the Old Name.

(If it is a new boat or a boat that never had a name, skip this step and go on to step three.)

Stand on or near to the bow of the boat. Say:

With the blessings and the authority of all that is divine throughout the universe, hear me and grant me permission to change the name of this good vessel. With that permission and blessing, I give thanks to God [or fill in what you feel is appropriate] as we set this name free. We do it with great respect and the utmost dignity. May it carry all our thanks and blessings with it.

[Old name of boat], you are released to the sea!

Step Three:

Have the balloon readily available and immediately set the balloon free into the air.

Step Four: Christening with the New Name.

Continue to stand at the bow of the boat. Have your flower petals in a bowl, bag, or container near you. You may want to cover them so they don't blow away. One person says:

May my/our blessings of safety and protection be carried to other vessels that journey upon these waters. And may their good blessings come back to this vessel three times three.

Take your flower petals and throw them into the water. (At this time, if you have other people who would like to participate, they, too, can throw flower petals into the water.)

Step Five:

Stand at the bow and stretch out your right hand. Turn in a 360-degree circle clockwise. As you do this, envision a sweeping white light that covers the entire boat.

Step six:

Say the following:

With the passion and the purity of angels, with the power and in the name of God [or whoever you feel appropriate], may this vessel be favored by the protective energy that mighty Neptune stands for. We offer thanks for the presence of all physical and nonphysical energies that grace this ceremony and their good intentions. We do these things in belief and faith. I christen this boat [new boat's name] . . . May she be blessed with calm seas, fair winds, and safe voyages for her and all her passengers.

Step Seven:

Have your champagne ready. Take the cork out of the bottle, place your thumb over the top, and shake the champagne. Spray the entire contents over the bow of the boat. Toast the boat with your extra bottle at this time if you choose.

In regard to boat christenings, as a form of protection, I must add a short testimony. A woman e-mailed me a thank-you for sending her this ceremony. I have copied it verbatim.

Dear Diane:

Thank you for the boat blessing ceremony you sent me. My husband and I performed it on our 35' Chris Craft two weeks ago. We had our boat at a marina here in Florida. There were 6 boats in a row at the dock, ours included. A lightning storm came up and blew the electronics out of every boat in that line. We were the only boat that did not receive damage!

Thank you,
Eleanor

Christening and Blessing for Pets or Miscellaneous Items

Step One:

Take a mixture of water and a pinch of salt and put them in a glass or glass bowl. Set it down and place both hands with palms down over the glass. Do not touch the glass.

Say: "May this water and salt be blessed with the energies of our creator. May it be energized with properties of protection and safety. And so it is."

Step Two:

Stand in front of whatever it is you want to christen or bless. Sprinkle just a bit of the water on the item. If working with a pet, you may want to rub the water on its forehead.

Say: "May blessings be bestowed upon you and keep you free from harm of any kind. May you be safeguarded by the powers that protect. In the name of God or [fill in the name of your higher power], I christen you [fill in the name]."

PART V

Daily Defense Systems

CHAPTER 21

Basic Daily Protection for You and Your Home

Every day we get out of bed, brush our teeth, comb our hair, and get dressed. These are all forms of protection. We are protecting our teeth from decay and our bodies from the environment. They have become habits and good ones. Another daily habit we should form is protecting our entire being from psychic attack.

Sometime, shortly after wakening every morning, stand up straight and encompass yourself with a blind of white light. I picture a white blind of light being pulled down from my head to my toes. It's quick, it does not take much thought, and if you are not a morning person, it does not overwhelm you. The very thought that at the beginning of the day you are aware you may fall victim to energy drain from numerous sources gives you a defensive edge.

Upon leaving your home, whether it is to go to your place of employment or to run errands, in your mind's eye quickly cover your abode with a circle of light. If you live in an apartment or condominium, cover the entire building. Don't be selfish by only protecting your unit. However, you may want to give your place a little extra boost by seeing the interior of your residence glowing with light as well.

As you continue throughout the day, you will constantly be receiving tiny forms of psychic attack. You step on someone's foot accidentally and they unintentionally throw a piecing dart. Your boss is giving you unflattering looks as he knows you were late for work . . . yet another dart. The waitress at the restaurant asks how your meal is and you tell her it was not cooked properly. Again a fragment of energy taken from you. By the end of a day you will find that people and situations can slowly chip away at your aura shield. You will not feel the effects immediately, but if you let them build up, you will once again find yourself tired for no apparent reason.

As a way to prevent this, you should renew your psychic shield daily in the middle of the afternoon if you feel it's necessary. When you start to feel you are lacking energy, sit down for a minute. Release through your hands the energies of those you have come in contact with.

Shake your hands at your sides as you would if you had writer's cramp. Imagine that as you shake your hands, the energy from all those people you have come in contact with is being removed. After you have shaken away the heaviness, visualize yourself in a glistening light.

As you need renewal throughout the day, so does your home. It cannot tell you about the hard day it had when you come home, but you may be able to feel the energy that is missing. It also gets psychic darts thrown at its structure.

If you live in a busy area, your home experiences cars honking, dogs barking, children crying, sirens screaming, and an entire array of attacks on its peacefulness.

If you live in the country, your home is still subject to intrusion. Birds or squirrels on the roof, the occupants slamming doors or opening windows, the wind blowing particles, and even something that may abruptly break, such as a gutter or screen. If you were to pay attention to the abuse your home receives daily, you would most likely have more respect for this structure that keeps you safe and warm.

At the end of your day when you arrive home or when you feel you are quieting down for the evening, renew the energy in your home. It is not necessary to go through any of the clearing procedures mentioned early, as those are meant for special occasions when you have specific concerns. What I recommend is an uncomplicated renewal of energy. Just like cleaning your house, if you keep up with it daily, you never have to perform major cleanup jobs!

If feasible, every evening go to your front door and stand facing the entry to your dwelling. Hold your arms out perfectly straight with palms facing up. With a slow lifting motion, move your hands upward and picture yourself lifting the energy from the floor straight out through the ceiling. The positive energy will stay in place and the unwanted energy the house has accumulated will be discharged.

Laughing: A Fun Way of Protection

An occult attack cannot take place when you are laughing. It is a discharge of energy that is very powerful. Your thoughts are occupied on such mundane issues that nothing can penetrate your presence of mind.

To illustrate my point, here is a situation that was presented to me some years ago: While traveling early one morning by train to downtown Chicago, a businessman sat down in the seat next to me. He commented that he hoped he would not fall asleep on the way there.

I asked him if he had been up late the day before. He expressed with surprisingly no embarrassment that he had a difficult time getting to sleep. "I always feel as though something is going to happen at night," he said, "or I think too much and just can't fall into a restful sleep." Naturally I recommended a different type of psychic self-defense that may have offered him comfort. He was open-minded to a point but nothing seemed to strike him as a solution he could understand or even want to attempt to try. Then I suggested laughing. This seemed to get his attention. He understood that when he was a part of anything humorous, he could not concentrate on anything else. However, he could not laugh the whole night through. "No," I admitted, "but you can go to sleep with humor on your mind."

I suggested he watch a nightly comedy show before he went to bed. This would serve as a type of protection from psychic aggressors. Also, he would go to sleep in a positive and lighthearted mode.

A few weeks later I saw the same man on the train. He said he had tried my suggestion and every day before bedtime watches a comedy program on television. I doubt if anyone could cast an evil spell on someone watching *Saturday Night Live* or *Monty Python*.

Laughter is a healer and a protector. Laughter can be stronger

than anger. Have you ever had someone laugh when you were trying to be serious? It can be infuriating and often you cannot break
through that energy. I am not suggesting you walk around town
laughing at anyone you dislike. But keeping a smile on your face
for people that annoy you can totally disarm their psychic war plan
and equally help protect you.

CHAPTER 22

Defense at the Workplace

Regardless of whether you work at a shopping mall, a hospital, an executive office complex, or the ballet, you must plan in advance your defense at the workplace. It is usually not your decision as to whom you will be working with or not, so you must do the best you can to guard yourself from psychic assault.

If you don't care for someone and your energies are not conducive, you must shield yourself as a way of withstanding the differences. Daily interactions with one or more coworkers who are not in synch with you can leave you fatigued by the week's end.

To save yourself from further weariness, you can always quit your job! However, assuming this is not the practical approach, I will offer you a resolution. We cannot force ourselves to like someone if we do not have it in our heart. We can tolerate them and be pleasant and avoid them as much as possible, but that is not always sufficient. We can still sense their energy and this is what we must consider.

Bear in mind, if you are aware that you and a fellow worker are not like-minded or you both are not traveling on the same plane on any level, that person most likely feels the same way.

A similar problem was related to me by a client.

Molly worked in an office in San Francisco. Her job was computer oriented and the cubical she claimed as hers was within ten inches of Jennifer, a coworker. Molly and Jennifer saw each other every day and sometimes had to work together on joint projects.

Molly always felt that Jennifer was condescending, and she looked forward to the days when Jennifer was not in the office.

Smiles went back and forth between the two women yet they hardly spoke. Molly was single and enjoyed her life. Jennifer was married, had three children, and had proof of it all over her desk.

Pictures filled every space that was not be occupied by a container of paper clips. This annoyed Molly because on occasion they needed to change desks and Molly would become annoyed as the pictures would fall down, flying all about the floor. There was nothing in particular that was a major problem between the two women, but Molly did not like being around Jennifer.

Then there was Steven. Steven, too, was getting on Molly's nerves. He worked in the legal department and she had to interact with him two or three times a day. He was happy and liked to wink at Molly. Molly could not tolerate the winking and ran every time she saw him coming down the hall.

Molly shared with me that there were at least seven people working on her floor who agitated her for no good reason. She was not paranoid or snobby, nor was she an unpleasant person by nature. She enjoyed her job and her social life was vast. It was just the people around her at work with which she could not seem to cope.

To most people observing, they would have found no specific cause for her dislike of her associates. The more she tried to accept them, however, the worse it became. In any other situation she could avoid people, but at work she did not have much of a choice.

I instructed her on how to perform what I call a "Soul and Personality Separation." She applied this mode of psychic defense and on the very first day she knew she had found her salvation. She now goes to work every day and enjoys everyone's company. She has more energy and on occasion even winks back at Steven!

If you are like Molly and find people at your workplace not to your liking, look outside this lifetime.

A Soul and Personality Separation

In order to have a successful "Soul and Personality Separation," you must follow a particular philosophy pertaining to past lives. That is, "You are what you were."

Without going into great detail, I believe that we not only evolve from one lifetime to another but we travel in "packs," so to speak. By this I mean that when you return to this planet to experience another life, you most likely knew the majority of people you interact with today.

That being the case, there must have been some earlier lifetime when you liked the people who now irritate you. To go back and carry out past-life regressions on all the people you work with is not the answer. However, to look past the personality of this lifetime is an excellent solution.

First, you must approach each person separately. Naturally, they will not know what you are doing as it will appear you are simply conducting a normal conversation. Strike up a conversation and try to make the subject not work related. The reason for this is that you will most likely not remember much of what was said.

Visually put a shield of white light (like a piece of glass) in front of their entire body. In this way you are blocking out their twenty-first-century personality.

In a matter of seconds, see them in another lifetime with a different personality. They could be male or female, young or old. You must think of what they were in a past life quickly. If nothing comes to mind, just guess. Think of it as a matter of life and death. What if someone said, within five seconds come up with a character from another lifetime and I'll spare your life! Out of desperation you would blurt out anything: nurse, barber, Indian chief, monk, prostitute! I'm sure you get the idea.

Once you have determined who they were in another life, sense if the person you knew then was someone you liked better than the one you see now.

If this is the case, think of the body standing in front of you as an actor playing a part in this lifetime. We have all seen our favorite actors play parts we don't particularly like. However, we know in reality no matter what part they are playing, we respect and admire them for their real-life personality. So is the case in people we have known from previous incarnations. We may not like their personalities in this lifetime but we always remember their souls.

Consequently, block each person's present-day personality with that shield of light and allow the soul of another time to shine through. You will be amazed at the difference it will make.

CHAPTER 23

Psychic Protection on Public Transportation

Travel today is fraught with anxiety and stress. Whether you are flying on a commercial airliner or riding on a bus or train, however you travel, you are constantly confronting, absorbing, and literally sitting in other people's energy!

Have you ever sat in a seat on some mode of transportation and got up and moved? You most likely recognized that something in that location was discomforting.

If you are sensitive to energies of both a positive and a negative influence, you most likely have developed a psychic agility. With this ability you can locate the best spot for you to be seated while traveling.

If seating is plentiful, you will not have a problem finding a comfortable place. Nevertheless, if there is only one seat available on the train, you have to make the best of the circumstances by clearing the seat from previous travelers' vibrations. If not, numerous energies may cling to your auric field.

I was visiting a friend in the hospital who was sharing a room with a woman who was there for various tests. She told me no one could determine the reason for her chronic headaches. For that reason, she was having tests done to determine a diagnosis.

After visiting with my friend, I conversed with her roommate for approximately twenty minutes. The woman told me she worked at a store quite a distance from her home. She added that it was far more practical and less expensive for her to ride the train to work than drive her car.

In making conversation, I asked what types of people rode the train. Were they business types, retired people, workers, or the creative kind? I was waiting for the usual answer that they were a variety of people from different walks of life. But to my surprise, she said they were mostly sick. Whatever did she mean, I thought, so I asked her.

She continued to tell me the particular train she rode stopped at two cancer treatment centers and one complex dealing with the visually challenged.

She had a heart of gold and saw good in the fact that people could travel a distance for treatment and did not have to drive or have someone drive them. Yes, I agreed, what a great location for these facilities and the convenience for the patients takes much pressure off these individuals.

Still and all, I knew their energy and the energy of their illness may linger in the area for some time. I am not implying you can acquire any type of illness from a train seat! What I am saying is that the vibration of fear, depression, ailments, and exhaustion can permeate a physical object such as a seat or bench. I had no scientific proof that this woman's headaches were coming from the vicinity of people using a given seat, but I could not help questioning this possibility in my own mind.

I could see she was good-natured, caring, and susceptible. To me this indicated a potential victim of unwilling psychic attack.

It can be very frustrating when you have information you want to share with someone, but are not sure how it will be taken. I took the chance and explained to her that I feel everything has a vibration that can be transferred on to us if we allow it to do so.

Energy, good or bad, can remain if not cleared. Luckily she listened with enthusiasm while I explained how to quickly clear a train, car, airplane, subway seat, etc. Anything that has been subjected to numerous people's energies should be freed from the previous rider or guest.

Without making a display of waving hand gestures or chants, I have devised a quick fix for public transportation.

As you walk toward your destination, focus on the space where you will eventually be seated. As there may be someone already sitting in the spot next to where you eventually will be, I do not recommend even the smallest hand gesture.

This could look curious or even frighten someone. Instead use your head and I mean that literally. Usually with the sweep of a hand you could clear that space, seeing the previous energy floating right out the window. However, when the public is involved, we must be very careful as to our actions.

Before you sit down, take your head and tilt it back as if looking at the ceiling. As you tilt your head back, think in your mind the word "leave." At the same time see your chin as a pointer that directs the energy from the previous occupant and all before him or her to depart through the roof of whatever it is you are traveling in at the given time.

Through intention and visualization you will achieve this easily. At the most, anyone that sees you will think you are just stretching your neck.

The lady in the hospital remembered what I told her and asked if she could have my phone number. She wanted to call me to tell me if it worked out. I did not hear from her for a long time and did not give it much more thought. I had shared my knowledge, and if it worked, it would have been wonderful, but if it did not, she would not have been any worse off than she was in the hospital.

Nearly two months later I got a call from some woman who said, "You were right!" As I have many clients I give psychic readings to, I could not imagine who it might have been. I finally confessed I was not quite sure who was calling. "It's me, the lady in the hospital, the one with the headaches."

To my delight, she told me she had used this method and the headaches slowly went away. The testing at the hospital had come up inconclusive. She still rides the train every day and says she always stretches her head before she sits down.

This method can also be used if you are in a situation where you are standing in a crowded bus or subway. Clear the space you will be using in the same manner.

CHAPTER 24

Scrolling Light for Dangerous Situations

A dangerous situation, no matter what it is, is not meant to be taken lightly. Please always use common sense and logic when you are at risk.

The scrolling light method of creating a psychic shield has been a great comfort to me in many situations. However, I utilize this only after I have taken all physical precautions and there is nothing left to be done.

In this case I will use myself as an example. I was at a concert in Tampa, Florida, with a friend. After the performance we proceeded to the underground parking lot where the car was parked. Somehow we left late and we were the only ones in the area. As we got into the car and started to drive away, an oncoming car started coming straight toward us. He was driving fast and we had nowhere to turn. We jumped out of the car and stood to the side as we saw him speeding ahead.

I covered the two of us, as well as the car, with a scrolling white light. All we could do was stand against a wall. Abruptly he hit his breaks, the car was saved, and we were safe. He immediately backed out and drove away.

In another instance, an astrologer I was consulting was advising me not to sign any contracts on a particular day. He provided me with a wealth of information and at the end of the reading told me there was no charge. This did not seem acceptable as he had no reason to wave the fee. I insisted I pay and he just said no, shaking his head. I had never seen him or talked to him before this appointment.

He would not explain the reason for this gift. As I believe there must be a fair exchange of energy for services, I could not walk away without paying him. Finally, he informed me that many years ago he had read a paper I had written for a client. It was not published in a magazine but just a handwritten explanation of how to use the scrolling white light method of protection.

The client had passed a copy on to him and he claimed it had saved his dog from disaster. I thought he was being overly dramatic and wanted to hear the story. The astrologer claimed that he was walking his new puppy on a residential street. The dog had a collar and leash but the collar was too large for the dog. The dog slipped out of the collar and ran into a busy intersection. As the man ran after his canine friend, he threw the scrolling light over the dog.

Traffic stopped and a woman got out of her car and grabbed the dog, bringing him back to his owner. The man was nearly in tears as he expressed his gratitude. Was it the scrolling light or just the way of the universe that saved the dog? Regardless, I thanked him for the reading and left.

This is a method of psychic defense against danger that should be used only in times of distress. If you use it too often, you will weaken the energy behind it. I hope you will never have reason to activate this technique.

Scrolling Light Defense

This technique must be executed within seconds. There is no time for preparation, rituals, ceremonies, or hardly even thought. The moment you feel you or someone else is in danger of any kind and you know all has been done to stay safe and there is absolutely nothing left but prayer and hope, employ this method. Pray at the same time if you like.

Visualize a tornado of white light swirling around you or whoever or whatever it is you are trying to protect. You will feel the chaotic forces, the confusion, and the blast of energy for a split second. But you will quickly be inside the tornado and protected by the powerful scrolling light that circles around you. Even if you stop visualizing the scrolling light, know it still exists. This should take you approximately three seconds to visualize.

After you are safe from your situation, you must see the scrolling light dissipate. Give thanks to the God of your understanding or your higher power. Anytime you overcome a disastrous situation, always remember to thank the source from which the light came.

CHAPTER 25

Gathering Places and Resistance

Attending a party or function for a festive occasion can be a delight. A funeral, a mandatory educational class, or an assemblage where we do not want to be can become draining.

People can bombard us with huge amounts of energetic forcefulness on both sides, positive and negative. Too much laughter and sweetness can be as debilitating as too much crying and sadness.

It is a challenge to deal with the liveliness or lack of liveliness from one person, let alone a group situation. At a gathering there is almost nowhere to hide from the variety of thoughts that fill the air.

When you attend anyplace where a group is assembled, you have entered into psychic chaos. The only few exceptions are meditation or spiritual groups or their equivalent, where everyone is asked to focus on one universal thought.

In a festive gathering, people are feeling not only happy but sad, jealous, tired, ill, frustrated, lonely, and any other emotion you can imagine. All these emotions spring back and forth across the room. They travel up and down, in and out. If you walk one foot away from a spot where you were standing, the energy of the room will most likely change.

This is why it can be tiring to attend a banquet or gala. It is not the food, beverages, dancing, or music but the people that tire us. Not even being aware you can come home with the anguish of Mark's divorce, the disappointment of Stan being fired, the joy of

Susan being pregnant, and the confusion of Anne being bisexual! Is it any wonder people say they don't have the strength to attend a group event?

Like it or not, there are those occasions when we will find ourselves among a group of people. To protect yourself psychically from each person attending is unfeasible if it is a large group. For this reason, you should exercise defense against the entire crowd and energize yourself with absolute psychic stamina.

As soon as you receive an invitation to a gathering, you should begin your plan of defense. Who is attending? What is the purpose? Are you excited about going or do you feel obligated? Once you have determined your attitude about the event, you can proceed. If you are eager for the function to take place, you are even more at risk of psychic attack. You may be so engrossed in what to wear, how your hair looks, and whether you can lose those last ten pounds before the gathering that you leave yourself open to all the forms of psychic assualt I have mentioned previously in the book. Try not to get so distracted with an event that you forget balance in your life.

On the day of the gathering, you will most likely be taking a bath or shower. Use this time to remove negative energy from your body. As I mentioned earlier, when something we normally do is done with a specific intention, it becomes a rite. Therefore, change your shower or bath the day or night of the event into a "rite" by thinking of it as a way of cleansing not only your physical body but your spirit as well. Wash the offensive vibrations that you have come in contact with that day off your being and see the water carry these vibrations down the drain.

After your "rite," take at least five minutes or more by yourself. Sit in a chair and relax. Imagine yourself not encompassed by white light but as an entire body of white light. It does not encircle you; you *are* white light. Instead of seeing flesh, you see radiant light. This will not only protect you but give you an energetic appeal when you enter a room.

This technique not only has freed people from potential psychic assault but has found many a single person a mate!

If you are going to be in attendance at a social occasion that is obligatory, use the same technique. The event may be a bit of a burden but the reception you receive will make the episode more enjoyable.

PART VI

Secret Realms Beyond the Physical (Cautions and Warnings)

CHAPTER 26

Astral Projection

Astral projection is the ability to detach the consciousness from the physical body. This allows the astral body to travel through time and space and then return without harm.

When you have separated your physical body from your astral body, the possibilities are endless. You can see yourself flying to any location in outer space or only to the house next door.

If you choose not to fly, you can simply just think about where you want to be. Your very thought can take you there in seconds. The location could be another planet or a friend's home in Australia. This is all done within moments and your physical body never leaves the room.

Many people also refer to astral projection as an OBE (out-of-body experience). This experience normally happens in a dream state. Some people naturally astrally project and don't even know what they are doing.

I have been astrally projecting since my early years. I was one of the lucky ones who did not know I was doing anything unusual until I read a book about the topic.

Some people find the entire idea difficult to embrace. Others are intrigued but frightened they will not come back to their bodies. For those who are fearful of leaving their bodies for a trip into the universe, I can certainly understand the concern. Hence, I have some tested remedies to make you feel safeguarded. Hopefully these ideas will provide you with sufficient comfort to encourage you to test this vast experience.

I will not assume at this point that everyone reading this book already knows how to astrally project. However, after enticing you to possibly attempt this voyage, it would only be fair to include at least one simple method for you to consider. This is a very uncomplicated process. There are many schools of thought on the subject that offer far more detailed instructions than I write on these pages. However, if you have a natural flair for such things, this may be all you need.

If you find the following method not specific enough, there is a lot of information at the library, on the Internet, and naturally at any bookstore that may better suit your understanding.

How to Astrally Project

You have the ability to astrally project any time of day you choose. However, this method is recommended for evening while lying in bed just before sleep. Before beginning your astral trip, try to remove as much jewelry as possible and wear comfortable clothing or night wear. The room should be as dark as possible, providing you are comfortable with the degree of darkness.

As sleep is approaching, you are already in somewhat of an altered state of consciousness. You have mentally started to relax and your body is also establishing calmness. This is a natural state, which allows you to surpass all the methods of acquiring deep relaxation through breathing techniques or self-hypnosis.

If you choose, you can take several deep breaths, inhaling and exhaling using the techniques you may already have practiced. However, I do not think this is necessary, owing to the fact you are already entering into a beta wave state.

Determine where you want to astrally project. Do you have a specific location or do you want to just travel and make decisions as you journey? Give yourself the mental suggestion that you will recall everything about your astral trip.

You should now lie on your back. Put your arms where they are comfortable—at your sides, crossed on your stomach, or wherever they naturally set themselves.

See yourself leaving your physical body. You are projecting up into the room; if you look down, you should be able to see your body as it is on the bed. You continue straight through the ceiling, over the roof of your home, and into the sky.

If you have determined you are going to a location on the earth, see yourself from the sky above your house projecting at light speed to that specific location. If you have never been to that location, just imagine it and you will find yourself there in seconds. When your have reached your destination, see yourself landing on the ground. For a few moments your surroundings may not be clear. However, with practice and time the images will become more vivid. At this time you are free to explore the place where you projected.

When you are ready, take yourself home the same way you arrived. See yourself coming back into the skies above your home, through the roof, into your room, and back into your physical body lying on the bed.

Your first trip will most likely be brief, because when you realize what you are actually doing, you will doubt whether it is possible or not. With these doubts you have limited yourself; hence, you will start to return home.

Fear may also play a part in a short excursion. As a form of protection to make you feel more secure, you can envision a silver "umbilical cord" attached to your body. By this method you will always find your way home, never getting lost or flung into space.

I have never used such a cord as I feel it would be confining. However, when first starting out, you may feel more comfortable and secure using one. Some people swear by the silver cord and would not attempt such a feat without it.

Also, make sure you are warm before you begin this session. Cover yourself with a blanket as your physical body tends to cool when you are astrally projecting. The cover is a form of shelter to keep your physical self safe. Another important thing I must point out is to always return the same way you entered, as this is the gentlest and most natural way to rejoin your body.

In the case of another person sleeping next to you or even in the same household, take caution. If you are suddenly disturbed by someone shaking you or touching you, you can come crashing down back into your body. This creates a shock to the system and brings you back too fast. A sudden impact can leave you feeling anxious or nervous for several hours afterward. You may even experience rapid heart palpitations. Normally, when you return in the proper manner, you should sleep for the rest of the evening and wake up refreshed with total recollection.

When I astrally project and I am not alone, I lock my door so as not to be disturbed, or I tell the person what I am doing and ask them not to touch me under any circumstances. If you are living with someone who is not open-minded to such ideas and you are not comfortable discussing your experimentation, you will have to work around the situation. Going into another room is probably the best solution. Always take all precautions.

The notion of astrally leaving your body may not be something you feel comfortable about. If even the very concept disturbs you, I recommend that you not investigate this activity.

I have heard many tales of astral projection and the results can be fascinating as well as disappointing. For instance, I was asked to substitute for a speaker at the last minute at a psychic convention early last fall. The subject I was to speak about was astral projection.

When I arrived at the podium, there was a larger group than I had anticipated. I was totally unprepared as I had only fifteen minutes to pull my thoughts together. However, I knew I could easily speak for thirty minutes on the subject, especially since I practiced it on a regular basis.

Right before I was introduced, the organizer informed me the lecture was to continue for an hour and a half. Thinking quickly, I decided to have an audience participation lecture and had several people stand up and tell about their failures and successes when undertaking astral projection.

It was at this session I heard some of the most interesting and, from what I could detect, truthful accounts of out-of-body experiences.

The one that comes to mind is the case of a man named Timothy. Timothy told the group that he had never attempted astral projection but purchased a videotape on the subject. After viewing the tape several times, he felt confident he would remember the procedure and was prepared to put forth the effort.

This particular tape suggested that the individual not picture himself floating up but flying through the air. Normally this is one of many methods in which several people have achieved great success.

The tape said nothing about including the use of a silver cord or any color cord for that matter. Timothy thought nothing of not having somewhat of a safety net, as the thought never crossed his mind. Tim had a great fear of flying in airplanes and always panicked upon takeoff and landing. However, he was not flying in an airplane and this flying was totally different. There was also a part of him that was not one hundred percent convinced that he could accomplish this task.

He lay on his bed with his eyes closed, and after counting down from one to ten with several inhales and exhales, he could feel his astral body rise! He said he was excited yet stayed focused. He flew through the roof and was suddenly outside among the trees and clouds.

Then, he said he did not imagine it, but to his surprise he saw an airplane coming at him. "I panicked," he told the audience. "I thought I would come crashing down into my bed but I didn't!"

He actually saw himself grab the wing of the airplane and hang on! The audience was roaring with laughter and I had to laugh as well. The gentleman continued to assure the audience he was not making up a story to amuse the crowd and I believed him.

He continued the account of his experience. It seems after he was flown around by what he now identified as a Boeing 727, the plane landed with him on the wing. He said he started to sweat and was totally confused.

He could not get back into the air although he tried many times to project himself upward. He jumped as high as he could several times but could not take flight.

"Finally," he said, "I don't know what happened but I was suddenly above my house looking down at the roof. I saw my body entering my bedroom and looked down at my physical body lying there peaceful and still.

"I was conscious again and covered with sweat. Of course I thought I experienced a combination of astral projection and a nightmare."

The next morning when he got out of bed, he felt exhausted. He knew he must have had a bad dream as the airport was miles away and very rarely did planes ever fly over his house.

Timothy managed a hotel at the end of town. Once at work he started to check on the guests that came in late the night before. He noticed an airplane pilot with a certain airline was booked.

As the pilot checked out later in the day, Timothy could not help but ask him a question.

"Flights don't pass over this area too often, do they?"

"Oh no," said the pilot.

Well, Timothy was again convinced he did not project out of his body and just fell asleep and had a bad dream.

"However," the pilot went on to say, "yesterday a 727 had to take a different route due to airway traffic." Timothy found out the plane must had flown over his house the same time he imagined himself astrally projecting. This still did not prove anything to him as he could have heard the plane in his sleep, causing these images.

The pilot continued and told Tim the other pilot had to stop at a local airport several miles away. The fellow flying the craft was a friend of the pilot telling the story.

As Timothy listened, he was also told that upon arrival, the pilot who landed the plane spotted a man jumping on the runway! "What happened to the man jumping?" Timothy asked. The guest said that when security arrived, they could not find the man.

From that point on, Timothy believed that astral projection was possible. However, he now uses the method of seeing a silver cord attached to his body so as to always be able to spring back home if necessary.

Another woman in the same crowd said she was always leery of astrally projecting because she did not like the idea of her body floating upward. I suggested she see herself walking through a door and the other side was exactly where she wanted to be. She could be in her bedroom one minute and walk through the door and be in England or on Venus the next.

I have also heard stories of people getting into astral fights with other projectors or beings and having terrible experiences. I feel if you do not look for trouble, you will not find any. Just as you have projected yourself to a location, you should be able to come back just as quickly.

When starting out, do not venture too far from home and work your way up. Have a destination as opposed to just wandering and your path should be clear.

In the case of Timothy, he did not have a set destination and I believe this was part of his problem. He was also traveling too slowly.

Astral projection is one of the most rewarding experiences I have encountered in metaphysics. If you have an authentic desire to develop this skill, you will no doubt continue to pursue it for many years to come.

CHAPTER 27

Astral Sex: Incubus and Succubus

What is an incubus and a succubus? These are astral entities who lie upon sleepers without their permission and have sexual intercourse with them—an incubus with a woman and a succubus with a man. Is it the lustful vitality of the victim that gives these beings their power? Modern medicine explains this away as a subjective impression produced by physiological disorders. But we must take into account as well the lower forces teaming with nonphysical entities that can take advantage of an unguarded person.

In medieval belief, it was considered a goblin who would have sexual intercourse with human beings. Their victims would assume they were having repeated nightmares when in fact it was thought to be real.

Incubi are sometimes spoken of as of either sex, male or female. However, an "incubus" is properly defined as a male, while a succubus is female. They are also known as vampires, ghouls, and demons.

In a case that came to my attention, an attractive middle-aged woman named Cynthia had visited a bed-and-breakfast establishment in Vermont with her husband. They had planned on a two-week business trip in the area. The town was small and this was the only lodging for miles. It was old and quaint and exactly what one might expect from this type of home. The owner was a jolly heavyset blonde with a strong religious background.

She did not believe in the existence of the paranormal or any-

214

thing that would make her question her own beliefs. This suited the couple fine, as they, too, had no interest in the supernatural. One night while sleeping, the wife had what she thought was a dream lover. Embarrassed, she said nothing and assumed it was an isolated incident. On the next night, the dream repeated. Cynthia never had a dream repeat itself and she thought this most curious. The third night she was reluctant to go to sleep, as she was becoming uncomfortable.

Finally she gave way to tiredness and fell fast asleep. However, this night what had been somewhat of a dream now took form as a nightmare. She was very aware of a male figure lying on top of her and forcing himself on her.

She could still feel the struggle when she awoke and was suitably exhausted. Her husband asked her what was troubling her and she explained she had a nightmare and it was nothing to concern him. These episodes continued for an entire week.

One day while her husband was attending a business meeting in town, she took a walk to a local park. A pleasant woman in her eighties sat down next to her on the bench. Cynthia started to fall asleep as she had been staying up nights as late as possible to avoid her nightmares. The elderly lady asked her if she was sick. Cynthia confessed she was having nightmares, but did not say what they were about. She went on to explain that she and her husband were staying at the bed-and-breakfast down the street.

The lady asked her if the nightmares involved any men. Cynthia was shocked and answered "yes." The stranger asked her if it was the same dream every night and if they became more disturbing. With great embarrassment, Cynthia confessed the entire ordeal.

The woman told her she could come to the bed-and-breakfast and protect the room for her. Cynthia was reluctant and wanted to know how she would protect her. The lady said she would draw a symbol of a pentagram on the doorway. No demons will pass under the pentagram. Cynthia declined the offer and decided she had made a great mistake talking to this woman. The next two days the bad dreams continued.

Again at the park Cynthia saw this woman. She tried to walk the other way but the lady caught up with her. "Still having nightmares?" Cynthia said no, which was a lie, and walked away.

That night for the first time in days Cynthia slept soundly without disturbance. The rest of the stay was delightful and everything was normal. Upon leaving, the innkeeper said to Cynthia that her friend had dropped her soap on the way out the other day. Cynthia had no idea what the proprietor meant. She handed Cynthia a bar of white soap. It was not unusual but merely a bar of plain soap. "You must be mistaken. I had no friend visit me," Cynthia commented.

"Well, I don't know who the woman was," the innkeeper continued, "but she seemed to go directly to the door of your room. I did not pay attention because I thought you were there." Cynthia was puzzled but made no account of the situation.

As the couple was getting into their car, Cynthia realized she had left a scarf over the sofa in their room. As she went back to collect it, she could not open the door. The owner had locked it so Cynthia called down the stairs for her to bring up the key.

As Cynthia waited in front of the locked door, she just happened to look up above the door. Very faintly she could see a pentagram drawn in soap above the door. She knew exactly why it was there and who had drawn it. Saying nothing, she collected her scarf and drove home with her husband.

Upon returning home, the exact nightmares started again and Cynthia was beside herself. Out of desperation one night when her husband was out of town, she drew a pentagram above the door. Again, as before, she was able to sleep, undisturbed.

She did not want anyone to see the pentagram, especially her husband. Hence, she covered the pentagram with a plate that hung directly over the symbol. This seemed to work. The pentagram was hidden from view and she never again had the same intrusive experience.

Are pentagrams the form of protection one should use to stop incubi and succubi? Some people speaking from experience tell me the answer is yes. I personally never had such an encounter and cannot say conclusively. I will tell you that the use of a pentagram as a form of protection is one of the best.

In another case a man who seemed to be attacked each night by a succubus displayed a cross and a pentagram with successful results. And as I mentioned in Chapter 7: "Possession and Walk-Ins," some people feel the use of the word "Jesus" is another way to avert such demons.

For these unusual cases I can offer only general advice and say try different approaches and see what works for you. However, if you think you are a victim of an incubus or succubus, I would also explore the possibility of a mental disorder and perhaps seek professional counsel. This is not saying that I do not believe in the reality of such entities. However, you should examine all possibilities before considering the supernatural.

CHAPTER 28

Remote Viewing

The subject of remote viewing has been debated for years. Some individuals consider it an out-of-body experience while others define it as a form of clairvoyance. By using visualization techniques, you have the ability to see a place, or view an event, without physically being present.

It is like watching live television. Your body stays in one spot but your astral body travels to observe a different location. Remote viewing and astral projection are similar but have their differences. Remote viewing is conducted while you are usually very conscious and many times while sitting up. A person will often draw a picture of what they are viewing as a way of experimenting and testing the accuracy of what they see. Also, you do not always imagine yourself leaving your physical body or floating.

Remote Viewing Experiments

As in any experiment involving astral travel on any level, you should incorporate a mode of protection before beginning. For remote viewing, I recommend a standard form of "white light" protection. Take a few seconds while seated comfortably and picture a gentle stream of white light coming down from above and entering your body through the very top of your head. It slowly spreads down your face, to your neck, shoulders, and arms to the very ends of your toes. See yourself becoming the white light as opposed to only being protected by the gentle radiance. You are the light and nothing can filter through. You are protected and in tune with your objective.

The easiest way to understand remote viewing is to experiment with it yourself. There are many ways in which to test your remote viewing skills. The ones I recommend will involve another person.

Method 1

Ask a friend to drive to an area a few minutes or so from your home, a place that you have most likely not visited. Do not ask them where they are going. You remain at home. Once the person is at their destination, have them take a photograph if possible. If you do not have a digital or instant camera, this step may be skipped.

By use of a cellular phone, ask your friend to call you to let you know you can now start your remote viewing process. Once you hang up the phone, close your eyes. Place yourself in an altered state of consciousness by breathing, counting techniques, or any method you normally utilize.

Draw a picture of what you think your friend is seeing. You do not have to be an artist or possess any artistic skills at all. If nothing comes to mind, just guess. You may see trees and buildings, or perhaps all you will imagine is a series of circles and squares. Do not try to be logical and think about what type of spot your friend may have gone to. It may be inside or outside; there are no rules. Just draw. As you are drawing, your friend should continue to stay at the "target" spot.

When you have finished, call your associate back and have them drive back to your home. Look at the photo and your drawing and see if you can find any similarities between them. Next, drive back to the "target" spot with your drawing and further compare.

Method 2

As before, protect yourself with white light. Have a friend drive to a location with which you would not be familiar. You must be in touch by cellular phone so as to know when you can begin. You, in turn, must be able to call back the person at the "target spot" so they know when they can leave and drive to the next location.

Place yourself in an altered state but this time see yourself sitting or standing right next to your friend looking at exactly the same thing he or she is observing. You do not have to see your body traveling as in astral projection. Just picture yourself with your friend. This time, however, do no drawing. Write down or tape-record what you think he or she is looking at that very moment. Describe as much as possible, for instance: birds flying overhead, earth-moving equipment, children playing, a large square structure, arches all around, and so forth.

When you have finished with one "target spot," have your friend drive to another location. Repeat this procedure five times at different locations.

When your friend arrives back at your home, have them listen to the recordings or read your written descriptions. See if they can match a recorded account of what you thought they were looking at, with a location they actually visited. Have them drive you to all five locations and see the results for yourself.

Note: The targets should be a variety of sites. Two different parking lots, for example, are too similar. The person going to the "target spots" should try to select locations as diverse as possible.

These experiments can also be performed with groups in which each person draws or writes down what he or she thinks the person at the "target spot" is seeing. Everyone can exchange results and the conclusions are always exciting.

Remote viewing can be interesting and fun. A good friend of mine who became very proficient at this technique used to keep track of her boyfriend's whereabouts by viewing where he was, whom he was with, and what he was doing.

One day while she was here in the United States, she conducted a remote viewing session to locate her boyfriend in England. She imagined him skiing with a blonde woman. The next day she called him and asked him "Who was the blonde" he was with the night before. His reply was, "Who told you?"

Some people feel that to remote view a situation in order to determine the whereabouts of someone else or some situation is not ethical if you do not ask permission. Obtaining permission is admirable on a personal level; however, remote viewing can go far beyond spying on a boyfriend or girlfriend.

It is said that the Central Intelligence Agency (CIA) conducted scientific evaluations of ESP abilities that included remote viewing. Unfortunately, some believe the conclusions in such studies were set before the investigations began! To prove whether such studies were successful or not is out of my range of time and resources and is not my professional goal. Numerous articles, Internet sites, and documented investigations are available if you want to further explore the actual findings on your own. However, most final results from a government standpoint are ambiguous and provide no actual positive conclusive evidence.

Whatever the truthful conclusions, if any government could master remote viewing, the impact would be phenomenal. The ability to view another country's defense methods or observe a classified government meeting with no one being in danger or physically present would change the mind-set of the planet.

No government would take the chance of military defeat, as there would be no element of surprise. Remote viewing could yield world peace! An interesting idea to contemplate.

Is remote viewing really possible and accurate? Anyone can develop this approach of astral voyaging. Remote viewing should not be judged until it has been tested personally by you. In this manner you will have firsthand information and personal results.

Protecting Yourself from Remote Viewers

We have addressed the benefits of remote viewing and methods with which to conduct these experiments. However, what about protecting yourself from someone who wants to remote-view you? Is there a means of defense so as to keep your privacy and a way of concealment? The answer is both yes and no. Yes, if you know someone will be visiting you via the astral plane. No, if it is not your intention to guard yourself from such an infringement daily.

Some people take the attitude that if someone wants to see what they are doing, so be it! This a very personal outlook. It probably depends on if you are doing something that another party may not approve of.

A good illustration of this, but I am in no way implying encouragement, is someone who is having an affair. If they were believers in remote viewing and knew their partner had developed this aptitude, they may be wise to mask themselves every time they were with their new lover. However, this method lasts only about twelve hours and needs to be refreshed if you mean to conceal yourself for longer. Just like with many things, it starts to dissipate with time.

Although different forms of white light projection are similar in technique each time you perform one, the intention must be focused and precise. You cannot very successfully cover yourself with a white light of protection once and expect it to cover everything from health to remote-viewing visitors. You must be specific. Therefore, if you feel someone will be trying to view you and a situation on a particular day, I advise the following.

Camouflaging Light Defense Method for Remote Viewing

When you feel the need to camouflage yourself from a remote viewer, you must visualize a foggy mist about your entire body. Do not become the light and do not merely see it encompassing yourself. See this for approximately thirty seconds and know it will remain for twelve hours.

If someone tried to locate you during that time via remote viewing, they would be somewhat disconnected. They could most likely sense your energy and see shadows knowing it was you, but would not be able to see clearly who you were with or what you were doing. For example, if you were in grocery store with people and merchandise around you, they could not visualize details. They may perceive you in a library, at a party, or a shopping mall. If you were embracing someone, they could not tell if you were carrying a package, holding a child, or scratching your back! Essentially you would be a blur and it would be a psychic drain for them to continue to deliberate your actions. Hence, they would retreat.

CHAPTER 29

Divination Safety
Approaches

Do not experiment with occult subjects about which you have no knowledge. Sometimes what you may perceive to be a harmless form of entertainment using a form of divination can turn against you and open you up for psychic attack.

Anytime you choose to use some material form of divining or predicting the future, such as tarot cards, Ouija boards, runes, pendulums, scrying mirrors, or such, you must protect yourself. You can easily fall prey to negative forces and nonliving entities that are just waiting to attack the unknowing student of the secret realms. Forms of divination are not games for Girl Scouts or just fun experiments for a bored couple. You are working and partnering with forces that can be either good or evil. It is my attempt in this chapter to direct you to the forces of good.

When I was about twelve years old, my mother told my sister and me never to bring a Ouija board into the house. When we asked why, she was very vague, to say the least. Naturally, we immediately went out, bought one, and hid it in the attic!

We read the instructions and started to watch the point of the needle. It spelled only gibberish. For me it was easier to read my cards if I wanted answers but I was determined to see what this was all about.

One evening I had my girlfriend Mary over, and she appeared to be quite an expert at consulting the "talking board." She had her own Ouija board hidden in her basement. Mary told me an elderly

Polish lady from Europe who claimed to be a mystic had taught her the proper way to use the board. Therefore, Mary was certain we would not conjure up any evil deities. I was not aware one could conjure up anything with a game. I just thought the nerves in your fingers moved the needle.

But after countless times exploring the Ouija board, I could see that some type of protection was needed. Mary and I were hearing strange noises that made no sense, as well as experiencing ill health, nightmares, and depression!

Was this the imagination of preteens? I thought so until I decided to throw away my Ouija board. Mother is always right! The day I put that board in the garbage can in the alley was the day my life took on a rosier outlook.

Believe it or not, I never used a Ouija board again until only a few years ago. However, this time I was prepared for battle.

I later learned Mary, who was now forty-one years of age, had also taken a path that related to metaphysics and still employed the forms of protection the European lady had taught her.

After purchasing a Ouija board from the local toy store (which in my opinion should not carry such a device), I started my experiments. At this point I was using it in solitude as I did not want to get anyone else involved.

I started to work with the board, and as in childhood, I could feel a mist of what I will describe as something sinister floating about the room. I did not want to be exposed to such a vibration and immediately put my board away.

The next day I used the precautions my friend suggested we apply years ago and they worked. I pass these on to you.

I will exclude the experiments I performed as this is not a book about how to use divination devices, but how to protect yourself when actually practicing them. I might also add that experimenting with such forces is not recommended unless you are well versed in this field.

To this day, I am still not personally a fan of Ouija boards as I feel the results are limited and time consuming. However, if used properly with the correct protection and patience, they can be very informative. Everyone has different experiences and what works for one may not work another.

Mary's Method of Protection with Ouija Boards

Light four white candles, which represent stability and good intention. Place them as close to the board as possible without getting in your way.

Do not consult the board at a solar or lunar eclipse. It is said that negative entities have easier access to the physical plane as these eclipses disturb the usual order of things.

Before you proceed, do not ask your higher power to be present, but only the good beings that will guide your hands on the board.

In a pleasant but firm way, get the message across that you are not interested in forces that are not of the light. You may say something like: "We ask only positive and loving spirits to be present here today while we consult this board."

Light sandalwood incense. Sandalwood is associated with protective qualities.

Visualize a white light around yourself and any other person present, as well as the Ouija board itself. See the room filled with a brilliant glow (Mary didn't add this part but I thought it was important). If you do not get answers or you are still picking up negativity, try again on another day.

When Using Tarot Cards

Tarot cards or any other type of cards that are read to predict future events or advise also have their own vibrational current.

- Before reading your cards, wash your hands. See any negativity you may have accidentally picked up being released down the drain of the sink.

- Now take your hand in a sweeping motion and clear the energy away from the last reading. Even if you were reading for yourself, you do not want lingering notions from previous predictions still present.

- Next cover yourself in a cloud of white light.

- Silently bow your head over the cards while holding them and say a mantra (sacred words, prayer, or chant). Ask that no unfavorable energy fall upon the room, yourself, or the querent (person being given the reading).

You may already have a protection technique you practice before "reading." If your methods are successful, there is no reason to substitute this one, unless you feel compelled to make a change. Remember, if something isn't broken, don't fix it!

Basic Defense Techniques for Divination

Pertaining to all the other forms of divination, I recommend a basic way in which to protect yourself and the querent.

Great care should be used when protecting yourself while using modes of divination. You are essentially opening up windows to the beyond and the mysterious. When you are engaging in divination, you are in an altered state of consciousness and prone to attack from not only the psychical but also the astral forces.

In the preceding pages I have discussed different forms of protection that may also be incorporated. However, foretelling the future, prophesy, and channeling are different in that you are allowing yourself to astrally travel into the future and dealing with potentially hundreds if not thousands of energies, entities, and forces to which we have probably not given names.

No one knows for sure what can invade our consciousness if we leave a window open. So the idea is, if you don't open the door, nothing will come through.

Before doing a reading of any kind, think about for whom you will be reading.

If it is you, there is no problem. If the reading is being given for a stranger, or the friend of a friend, you must act with all caution. Is this person serious, a skeptic, or neither? Out of the three, the most protected person will be the skeptic.

This may shock some, but a skeptic is so opposed to such things that his or her energy by nature will redirect any potential psychic aggression back at the person sending it. They don't even know they have achieved such a feat.

Someone serious or open-minded to the paranormal is more

vulnerable as they are willing to investigate the ethereal and psychic phenomena. The fact that they are allowing the universe to "show them what it's got" opens them up to psychic attack.

It reminds me of a country person going to New York for the first time. It can be frightening yet exciting. They will find wonderful things they may never have known existed. However, at the same time if they are not aware of the dangers and do not practice all manners of caution, they could possibly get hurt. It is for this reason we must protect other people we are "reading for," as they may not be aware of the consequences.

Divination Protection Technique: White Rain

Take a moment of silence once you and the querent are seated. This can apply to any type of divination. If you are reading for someone else, it is not necessary to discuss the details of your protection technique unless you so choose.

Envision a white rain coming down from the ceiling, falling gently on you and the querent. The motion of light in the form of rain is active, and the movement confuses and repels negativity from crossing through to you and anyone else you have protected. The warm white rain will descend for the entire time of the session. When you are finished, see the rain slowly stopping until it is there no longer.

I have used this method for the twenty-some years I have been performing readings. To my knowledge, it has never let me down. I always feel safe and protected, and energies that I have not wanted to encounter have never knocked at my door during a reading.

Conclusion

We have spent time together through the pages of this book. In some areas I have provided great detail, and in others much is left to your own inclination as I provided only the basis with which to start. Typically the concept of psychic protection is not the starting point for those new to metaphysical concepts. Therefore, I must presume my readers already have some knowledge of the occult, New Age thought, and psychic research and already have started their own spiritual journey.

I have addressed issues that are related to health both mentally and physically. It is here that I must express a disclaimer. The methods in this book are by no means meant to diagnose or substitute for professional medical or psychological advice. I have provided thoughts and theories from my own life's experiences, as well as those I highly respect.

You will find that my rituals and ceremonies are basically nondenominational, which is my intention. Some have echoes of Wicca attached to them and others a great deal of Christianity. I address many Chinese beliefs and express respect for the ways of the Native American. However, most ideas are the sum of many belief systems.

These are methods and practices that have been used with great success by myself and numerous others who have taken the time to venture through these practices and are not meant to reflect one specific belief system.

As you hold this book in your hands, I personally wish for you blessings and protection by the "White Light" that shines within you, around you, and above you.

GLOSSARY

Affirmation: A positive declarative statement about yourself, asserting that what you wish to achieve is already occurring.

Astral Projection: An out-of-body experience in which the astral body can travel to anywhere in the universe.

Altered State of Consciousness: A trance-type state in which the conscious mind is subdued and the subconscious has freedom to direct you. The operation of any psychic skills is performed in an altered state.

Amulet: A small object usually worn around the neck thought to have the power to protect the wearer. Amulets contain religious symbols, stones, and coins or may have an inscription or figure engraved on it.

Apparition: The sudden and unexpected appearance and disappearance of a ghost or nonliving entity.

Aromatherapy: A method of holistic healing using volatile plant oils including essential oils through inhalation or massage to promote physical and psychological well-being.

Astral Body: The spiritual counterpart of the physical body sometimes called "body of flight." A second nonphysical energetic body that has the ability to leave the physical body for an out-of-body experience while a person is sleeping or in an altered state of consciousness.

Astrology: The study of how events on earth correspond to the positions of the sun, moon, planets, and stars. Astrologers believe that the position of planets at the exact time of a person's birth reveals their character and their destiny.

Aura: An energy field that surrounds all physical and astral bodies. Our auras have colors associated with them that can be seen by "sensitive people" or special photography. As our emotions change, so do our auras.

Black Candle: A candle used in ceremonies or rituals to dispel negativity from our lives. As the blackness of the candle burns down, so does the negativity around us.

Chakras: Sanskrit for wheels or disks. The seven major spinning energy centers of the body, starting from the tailbone to the top of the head.

Chanting: A word or phrase repeatedly spoken in a simplistic singsong intonation. Chanting is often used in spiritual and religious ceremonies to induce trance states.

Clairaudience: An extrasensory ability to hear things beyond the range of the physical ear. Psychics that hear messages from the dead are known to be clairaudient.

Clairsentience: Translates from the French "clear sensing." The ability to perceive something without using physical senses.

Clairvoyance: The ability to see people, places, or things not in the same location you are located. Many intuitives describe themselves as clairvoyants as they can "see" future events before they happen.

Curse: A conjuration placed on a person or people with the intention of bringing harm or "bad luck" into their life.

Divination: The practice of foretelling the future by use of psychic tools, such as tarot cards or other occult means.

Evil Eye: A harsh look of hatred or a curse delivered telepathically by an individual who has supernatural power.

Feng Shui: The Chinese art of placement. An ancient philosophy that works with the balancing of energy or ch'i. The system strives to achieve harmony with spiritual forces believed to influence the environment in our homes, workplace, or surroundings.

Hex: Usually associated with black magic. A ceremony or ritual where a representation or effigy of a person is used as a means to inflict evil intention to the victim. For example, a voodoo doll is used in a hex.

Incubus/Succubus: An incubus is a male nonphysical entity sometimes thought to be a demon that has sexual intercourse with women while they are asleep. A succubus is the female counterpart that is said to "lie upon" men while the men are sleeping.

Mantra: Sacred words such as a prayer or chant that are repeated during a meditation or rite to facilitate spiritual power.

Meditation: Concentration of one's thoughts on a single intention or the illumination of all thoughts for the purpose of spiritual development and relaxation.

Mental Telepathy: A form of communication between two people without the use of speech, writing, or any physical factors. Thoughts travel from one person's mind to the mind of someone else.

Mudra: A spiritual hand gesture that has mystical power. The way in which you position your hands in times of prayer, meditation, or ceremony.

Ouija Board: A game involving two people that uses a planchette and a board to answer questions and give messages. Some believe the messages come from beings not of this world or the deceased. Each person gently sets his or her fingertips on the planchette. A question is posed and the planchette moves throughout the board, stopping on a series of numbers, letters, or the words "yes" or "no."

Out of Body Experience (OBE): The experience in which a person's astral body departs from their physical body, enabling them to observe the universe from a view not of the physical.

Paranormal: Psychic or mental phenomena that cannot be explained or understood in the terms of scientific knowledge.

Pendulums: A weighted device attached to a string or chain that one can make or purchase to receive messages from one's inner self. It is used as a form of divination to predict future events or to make decisions when uncertain.

Poltergeist: A noisy spirit. A ghost that is known to be restless, creating noises and moving objects to disturb home dwellers.

Psychometry: The ability to obtain information or tune into a person's vibration by touching an object that belongs to that individual.

Reiki: A form of treatment in alternative medicine in which energy is used as a healing modality. The energy is channeled from the Reiki practitioner to the patient for numerous healing affects such as reducing pain, adding vitality, and relieving stress.

Remote Viewing: An out-of-body experience that allows you to see people or places without physically being present.

Runes: An ancient Germanic alphabet used for writing and foretelling the future. An oracle in which one can ask advice and questions. A symbol is etched on a stone or chip. The stones are thrown or chosen and the "reader" interprets the message.

Scrying Mirror: A black mirror used as a tool for "seeing" past, present, or future events.

Seance: A meeting usually involving two or more people for the purposes of communicating with the dead. Typically a medium, a person who has the ability to communicate with the departed, is present to conduct the process.

Specter: A ghost that haunts repeatedly. Usually they reveal themselves over time and not immediately.

Spell: A formula that uses spoken, written, or chanted words for the purpose of creating an end result that may pertain to anything one wants in life. Some spells include special items such as candles or herbs.

Spirit Guides: Positive individuals who used to have physical form but have passed on to the other side and have chosen to help and aid the living. They can be relatives who are deceased or total strangers who are well versed in the area in which we need guidance. Spirit guides should not be confused with angels, as angels never had physical form but were created as angels.

Synergy: The combined energy of two or more people or things, which are greater than the sum of their individual effects.

Talisman: An object that has been given magical properties and will give the person that carries or wears it special powers.

Tarot Cards: A deck of seventy-eight special cards used as a form of foretelling the future. The cards include symbols and imagery that appeal to the "reader's" subconscious mind, bringing forth insights and predictions. Many psychics perform "tarot readings" as their source of divination.

Third Eye: The astral eye, one of the seven chakras, located in the center of the forehead. Often said to be an eye of intuition that on most people is not open.

Visualization: The creation of a vivid mental image one may utilize for the purpose of well-being, creativity, psychic journeys, personal development, and spiritual pursuits.

Walk-Ins: A soul we have agreed to let walk into our living body as we choose to have our soul walk out.

White Light: A spiritual shield that can be visualized in different forms to protect oneself from encounters with various living and nonliving energies.

Wicca: A legal, nature-based religion and a modern form of witchcraft. Wicca is *not* a Satanic religion. Wiccans perceive Deity as male and female: the god and the goddess. Wiccan creed states, "As it harm none, do as ye will." Wiccans respect the planet, themselves, and other people.

BIBLIOGRAPHY

Abell, George O., and Singer, Barry. *Science and the Paranormal.* Charles Scribner's Sons, New York. 1981.

Andrews, Ted. *How to Uncover Your Past Lives.* Llewellyn Publications, St. Paul, MN., 1992.

Arnold, Larry, and Nevius, Sandy. *The Reiki Handbook.* ParaScience International, Harrisburg, PA. 1982.

Biedermann, Hans. *Dictionary of Symbolism.* Facts on File, Inc., New York. 1989.

Cayce, Hugh Lynn. *Venture Inward.* Paperback Library, New York. 1964.

Denning, Melita, and Phillips, Osborne. *Creative Visualization.* Llewellyn Publications, St. Paul, MN. 1980.

———. *Practical Guide to Psychic Self-Defense & Well Being.* Llewellyn Publications, St. Paul, MN. 1980.

Dunwich, Gerina. *The Magick of Candle Burning.* Carol Publishing Group, Secaucus, NJ. 1989.

Essential Oils Desk Reference. Essential Science Publishing. 2000.

Fortune, Dion. *Psychic Self Defence.* The Aquarian Press, London. 1930.

Gray, Eden. *A Complete Guide to the Tarot.* Crown Publishers, New York. 1970.

Greenhouse, Herbert B. *The Book of Psychic Knowledge.* Taplinger Publishing Co., New York. 1973.

Hoffman, Enid. *Develop Your Psychic Skills.* Para Research, Gloucester, MA. 1981.

The Holy Bible. New International Version. Zondervan Publishing House, Grand Rapids, MI.

Hope, Murry. *Practical Techniques of Psychic Self-Defense*. St. Martin's Press, New York. 1983.

Howard, Jane M. *Commune With the Angels*. A.R.E. Press, Virginia Beach, VA. 1992.

Kennedy, David Daniel. *Feng Shui for Dummies*. IDG Books Worldwide, Inc., Foster City, CA. 2001.

Phantom Encounters. Time-Life Books, Alexandria, VA. 1988.

Pickands, Maracia L. *The Psychic Self-Defense Personal Training Manual*. Samuel Weiser, Inc., York Beach, ME. 1997.

Richards, Steve. *The Traveler's Guide to the Astral Plane*. The Aquarian Press, Wellingborough, Northamptonshire. 1983.

Rossbach, Sarah. *Feng Shui, The Chinese Art of Placement*. E.P. Dutton, Inc., New York. 1983.

Rossbach, Sarah. *Interior Design With Feng Shui*. Arkana, Penguin Group, New York. 1987.

Search for the Soul. Time-Life Books, Alexandria, VA. 1989.

Silbey, Uma. *The Complete Crystal Guidebook*. U-Read Publications, San Francisco, CA. 1986.

Sullivan, Kevin. *The Crystal Handbook*. Penguin Group, New York. 1987.

INDEX

ABOUT THE AUTHOR

Diane Ahlquist is a third generation psychic and spiritual counselor born in a suburb of Chicago and currently living on the West Coast of Florida. Her experience and knowledge stem from a lifetime of study and experiences beginning from childhood.

She has contributed as an advisor in the paranormal for film, television, and literary works. Practicing several forms of divination, she has aided in various types of investigative work throughout the country. Diane also lectures at seminars throughout the United States and acts as a facilitator for spiritual retreats.

Psychic phenomena is a constant exploration for Diane as she continues to write on topics that reach beyond the limits of the five senses.